HARVESTING, PRI

ARTISAN *New York*

PRESERVING & ARRANGING

DRIED FLOWERS

Cathy Miller

PHOTOGRAPHS BY ROB GRAY

EDITOR: Siobhán McGowan
TEXT EDITOR: Eleanore Lewis
DESIGNER: Susi Oberhelman
PRODUCTION DIRECTOR: Hope Koturo

Published in 1997 by Artisan,
a division of Workman Publishing Company, Inc.
708 Broadway, New York, NY 10003

Library of Congress Cataloging-in-Publication Data
Miller, Cathy
        Harvesting, preserving, and arranging dried flowers /
Cathy Miller : photographs by Rob Gray.
        p.   cm.
    ISBN 1-885183-51-8
    1. Dried flower arrangement. 2. Flowers—Drying.
3. Flowers—Collection and preservation. I. Title.
SB449.3.D7M57   1997
745.92—dc21   97-15287
                                         CIP

PRINTED IN JAPAN

10 9 8 7 6 5 4 3 2 1

First printing

DEDICATION

This book is dedicated to my husband, Charles, and my daughters

Mary and Catherine, whose love, support, and gardening assistance have

enabled me to write about one of my great loves...dried flowers.

THE DESIGN

Part three

APPENDICES

ACKNOWLEDGMENTS

DEEP APPRECIATION IS DUE my text editor, Eleanore Lewis, who always had faith in my capabilities and with whom I had the pleasure of working over the years while she served as gardening editor for *Family Circle* magazine and later as a gardening editor for Woman's Day Special Interest Publications' gardening magazines. I am proud to include her among my favorite "gardening people."

Thanks are also due to my first supporter, Orrin Macy of *Family Circle*, who introduced me to the magazine flower world, and to Deborah Harding, who accepted my first dried flower article for publication in *Family Circle*. Others in the magazine field who were pleased with my creative endeavors included, to name a few, Florine McCain of *Victorian Decorating* and Marie Walsh of *Christmas Helps* magazine.

Outside the writing field, my heartfelt thanks are directed at the late Rusty Young, Chief White House Floral Designer, and Rex Scouten, Curator of the White House, for all their assistance and kindness. They helped make my White House endeavors a dream come true.

To my photographer, Rob Gray, a talented and caring gentleman, whose efforts helped capture the beauty of my flowers, I am deeply grateful.

To the many friends and fans who have accompanied me "down the garden path" and into the world of dried flowers, my sincere thanks. In this regard, I would like to mention a few to whom I am especially grateful: Delores Spoor, Jim Twilliger, Ruth Krobetzky, Joe Vasile, Ellen Berger, Mrs. Frances Franzcyk, Ken Norman, Joyce Dykstra, Wayne Davis (president of Flower-Dri®), and the Wyckoff Garden Club members.

In addition, special thanks are due my demonstration/lecture assistants over the years: Pat Leahy, Maryann Sellers, Diana Schopen, Muriel Williams, and, for the past seven years, my faithful friend Ronnie Cangialosi.

I would also be remiss not to mention the constant, loving support of my two sons-in-law, Peter Egan and Tom Jones, my brother John Peragallo and sister-in-law Christine, and my adorable granddaughter, Tavia (my "little lovey"), whose youthful enthusiasm for gardening and flowers keeps me inspired.

Lastly, undying appreciation to my late devoted parents, who blessed me with their artistic talents for music and growing flowers and who instilled in me the profound belief that "you can accomplish anything you set your mind to, with hard work and God's help."

Thanks are also due to the following, who offered their homes as settings for some of the photographs in this book: The Hermitage, a national historic landmark in Ho-Ho-Kus, New Jersey, Florence Leon, Executive Director; Robert and Alyson Mitchell, of Wyckoff, New Jersey; and Rex and Rona Shaw, of Ridgewood, New Jersey.

INTRODUCTION

Within each of us lies a garden,
you need only look inside,
It lies within our hearts,
where love and hope abide.

GINA LAURIN

TO BE BLESSED WITH THREE great loves in my life—flowers, music, and family—leaves me deeply grateful and somewhat spellbound.

As a toddler, I was introduced to the wondrous beauty of flowers and gardening by my mother, Tavia, and my grandmother, Catherine. My grandmother taught me the common names of the flowers in her extensive gardens long before I mastered my ABC's. She provided a small space in her garden for me to call my own and tend to whenever I visited, which was quite often. The realization that nature and human beings could produce and prolong "things of beauty" fascinated me, and a bond formed that very first summer.

My mother, on the other hand, encouraged me to "pick a few" for the kitchen table and organize them as I saw fit. This freedom of expression was fueled by actual visions of finished arrangements—a gift my mother possessed as well. This blessing, as I call it, has enabled me to capture many top awards without any formal training in floral design.

Situated among acres of flowering fields, a gazebo at the Miller farm in upstate New York provides the perfect resting place, and offers some shade from the midday sun.

The love for flowers and gardening was an important part of my early childhood, and it was coupled with a love of music when I was featured in my first piano recital at seven-and-a-half years old. Since Mother was a concert pianist and Dad played by ear (and founded a pipe-organ company), it was natural for me to pursue and enjoy the concert stage, which I did through my 16th birthday. I recall vividly the excitement I felt when I would receive gorgeous bouquets after each recital. Their backstage beauty often overshadowed the effects of the applause, and more than once my brother, John, would exclaim, "Put those flowers down, Kate, and hurry out on stage for another bow!"

The pendulum swung from music back to flowers some 20 years ago, when my husband, Charlie, and I purchased a 33-acre farm in upstate New York. It is situated on a sunny, picturesque mountaintop with rich, loamy soil. As my eyes surveyed the landscape for the first time, I remarked to my husband and daughters, "What a perfect spot for a *little* garden!" They often remind me of this statement, because the garden space has grown larger every year since. To add more fuel to the fire, the farm was purchased primarily as a place where my husband could escape the pressures of business. Little did he know then that he would be kept busy plowing, spreading manure, building rock walls, and digging fence posts!

My prediction proved correct, and, before long, gorgeous flowers were blooming everywhere. That "little garden" had expanded into five impressive pockets of color.

Next entered my third love—family. Without the cooperation and support (both emotional and physical!) of my husband and two beautiful daughters, Mary and Catherine, the vast gardens could never have evolved. Even my young granddaughter, Tavia, is involved; she delights in planting seeds and wiring strawflowers.

Flawless blossoms in abundant quantities piqued my interest in the art of flower-drying. Back then, I never imagined that the methods I had developed would be passed on to thousands of dried-flower enthusiasts through dozens and dozens of magazine articles, lecture/demonstrations, television and radio appearances—and now this book! Having been blessed with the support of a wonderful family, I have pursued my dream of a lifetime and realized a "hobby gone crazy."

Let me backtrack a little....

It all began while I was a member of the Wyckoff Garden Club in New Jersey, when I entered the New Jersey State Flower Show. I was awarded the Creativity Ribbon for my dried garden-flower submission entitled "The Governor's Entrance Hall." This large, full arrangement contained delphiniums, 'Silver King' artemisia, peonies, crested cockscomb, strawflowers, and roses. It was seen by Orrin Macy, of *Family Circle* magazine, who admired my work and arranged an interview for me with the magazine's crafts editor. The result was a six-page article on dried flowers, complete with pictures and timing chart (*Family Circle*, June, 1976).

That feature caught the eye and the interest of Rusty Young, Chief White House Floral Designer, who contacted me and asked me to bring two dried flower arrangements to possibly augment the fresh arrangements in the White House. Three months later, during the Carter administration, I was invited to spend a week creating the first ten, of many, dried flower designs for the White House. Mr. Young commented that my dried flowers were so true to life they could pass for fresh.

I was shown around the White House by Mr. Young, who indicated places where my designs would be positioned and presented the vases to be used. On the spot, I had to absorb the decor and combine it in my mind with an appropriate creation. I decided on mass designs in Victorian shades of magenta, purple, and pink, which were perfect for the settings and the mostly blue carpeting. During the Carter years, I completed 28 arrangements. I also did arrangements during the Reagan (lots of reds) and Bush (blues) administrations.

For President Clinton, however, I made special dried arrangements under glass—because he suffers from allergies. One of the glass containers was originally a doll showcase. I glued a three-inch-square block of florist's foam to the center of the base; the central, spiky flower was inserted first, to establish the proper height; and the base ferns and flowers were kept an inch from the outer edge. All the flowers were wired for flexibility and security. The arrangements are viewed from all sides and sealed under the glass, which is secured to the base with a few drops of craft glue. Kept away from direct sunlight, and protected from dust, humidity, and possible pet problems by the glass, they will be perfect for years of enjoyment.

As of spring 1995, I had completed 56 dried flower arrangements for the White House, from Carter to Clinton.

Though it was difficult for me to imagine that anything could be more exhilarating than my White House work, I truly believe it happened in the Vatican in 1982, the year Charlie and I celebrated our 30th wedding anniversary by vacationing in Italy. I had prepared a five-by-seven-inch shadow box arrangement under glass, containing pink sweetheart roses, forget-me-nots, larkspur, and dainty white ammobium and feverfew in a Victorian-style bouquet. It was my intention to present this gift to the Pope during our visit. Circumstances beyond belief occurred: I got passes to the Pope's only appearance that week, on St. Patrick's Day; I was able to get a seat on the aisle in the auditorium; and the Pope came right over to me, my outstretched hands holding the picture frame. Taking hold of it, he said, in perfect English, "That is *so* beautiful—they are *real* flowers?" "No, Your Holiness," I replied. "They are homegrown dried flowers." He again proclaimed, "They are so beautiful," and, with his right hand touching my forehead, said, "May God bless you and your flowers." Then he walked away with the picture.

Nothing can compare with that experience. But my television appearances —on such programs as "The Joe Franklin Show" and Bill Boggs' "Saturday Morning Live"—fortified my belief that there is tremendous interest in dried garden flowers. This has been further verified in responses to my magazine articles, especially those featured in Woman's Day Special Interest Publications' gardening magazines and *Victorian Decorating,* where my gardens and flower arrangements have been pictured. Reaching flower lovers with my lecture/demonstrations will always be very rewarding to me. Truly, it was the constant encouragement of my "fans" that led me to write this book—to spread the love of dried flowers.

It is my hope that the advice and the "recipes" provided in this book, along with the vivid accompanying photographs, will start you on the same hobby of flower-drying (although perhaps it will not be as all-encompassing as mine has become). In addition, I hope that you will derive joy from preserving some garden flowers in pleasing displays to refresh your memory throughout winter months. I can guarantee a new peace of mind and a greater appreciation for nature's beauty through dried flowers.

Cathy Miller

part one

THE HARVEST

Chapter One

FROM DIRT TO DAHLIAS

'Twould be to me an honor,
If where your garden grows,
I could but be a daisy—
That stands beside the rose.

DIANA SUE LINDLEY

IT HAS OFTEN BEEN SAID that "a garden doesn't grow in a day." True, and in spite of the time it takes to cultivate a garden, its beauty is ultimately fleeting. In keeping with nature's cycles, flowers bloom, then fade. Every garden is a dream in progress, and every gardener a beautiful dreamer, determined to nurture, coddle, and coax tiny seedlings out of the soil each spring. The gardener's dream can be perpetuated through the art of preserving flowers.

A garden requires the most basic of ingredients: a plot of land, a patch of sun, a scattering of seeds—then just add water! In the absence of these essentials, fluorescent or grow lights, commercial mulch, terra-cotta containers, and so on, can be substituted. While each flower has its own individual needs, plants in general adapt themselves to all sorts of situations. For the gardener, it's simply a matter of practice and of patience. As with any other relationship, this one needs time to grow.

With their characteristic cupped petals and bobbing flower buds, poppies put a happy face on any garden.

BEGINNING 🌿 In order to create a healthy, radiant garden, it's essential to provide the proper growing conditions. A bright location—one that receives at least six hours of direct sunlight each day—is particularly important for the types of flowers that are the best candidates for drying. If your yard lacks light but you're determined to grow and dry flowers, consider finding a neighbor who has a sunny yard and "cultivating" a friendship!

After you have found a spot—part of an existing garden, perhaps, or an entirely new area—enrich the soil with liberal amounts of well-rotted manure or compost. I'm lucky to have an abundance of manure from the dairy farm next door, but you can use any commercial (relatively scent-free) brand of compost or composted cow manure. If your soil is sandy or full of clay, add peat moss to improve drainage.

ARTFUL COMBINATIONS 🌿 Gather together an assortment of seed catalogs and scour the everlastings sections, then the annuals and perennials, for plants that appeal to you. (Everlastings in particular, with their papery petals, retain their color and form when dried. In addition to the popular pearly everlasting, everlastings include acroclinium, ammobium, globe amaranth, and strawflower.) Next, sketch out your ideal garden on a sheet of plain or graph paper. Take note of the mature heights of the selected plants and position them in the bed to form a pleasing, graduated wall of color. Low-edging plants, such as floss flowers, button zinnias, and dwarf marigolds, make a picturesque outline for the garden and also dry very well. Blend groups of colors so that they complement one another.

My favorite way to design a garden is to plan it around a focal point: a weathered wooden bench nestled under a flowering crab apple tree; a romantic Victorian gazebo; a trellis covered with clinging wisteria. This way, an otherwise simple garden takes on an appealing look, inviting visitors to explore and enjoy nature's bounty—to stop and smell the roses.

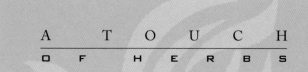

A TOUCH
OF HERBS

Wherever you situate your herb garden—here, at right, it's nestled amid the curved stone foundation walls of a former barn and milk house, near an old water pump—plant it informally, in scattered groups rather than in rows. Herbs—chives, lavender, and oregano—mingle with black-eyed Susan, orange trumpet vine, climbing bittersweet, pastel yarrow, and Queen Anne's lace. Because these are all perennials, the only planting required each year is of an assortment of annual flowers that mirror the red on the pump handle—in this example, crested cockscomb and zinnias. The nearby mountain ash tree completes the setting with its airy, spreading branches and, in fall, its colorful orange berries.

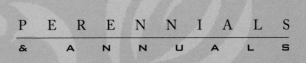

PERENNIALS
& ANNUALS

A lush, abundant garden, such as the one pictured at left, contains the perfect variety of flowers to insure maximum color and form when dried. To incorporate the garden into a pre-existing landscape design, set it off with a fence and plant outside as well as inside the borders. Low-growing annuals and perennials form a carpet of color outside the fence. A rustic trellis over the gate supports wisteria and silver lace vine. A focal point, such as the Victorian urn filled with flowers and cascading, variegated vinca vine, adds to the charm.

For a garden of approximately 25 by 40 feet, plant in rows inside the fence, much like an old-fashioned cutting garden. Space rows one foot apart to make them easy to cultivate. When the plants eventually "merge" together, they'll create a solid, pleasing mass of color that also discourages weeds from growing.

Along the rear of the fence, delphinium, foxglove, hollyhock, and phlox form a wall of flowers. The inner garden consists of cockscomb, cosmos, globe amaranth, green amaranthus, larkspur, marigold, snapdragon, and zinnia (all annuals), plus black-eyed Susan, coneflower, German statice, gloriosa daisy, Japanese peony, liatris, pearly everlasting, and Shasta daisy (all perennials). Outside the fence, annuals ageratum, dwarf dahlia, petunia, and verbena are interspersed with perennials 'Silver Mound' artemisia, coneflower, and campanula.

Garden Tours
50¢

For a small but very colorful annual garden, plant dahlia-type 'Tetra' zinnias, crested 'Red Velvet' cockscomb, tall strawflowers, and a variety of different sunflowers. Add larkspur and ammobium for touches of cooler blue and white. A garden such as the one pictured below requires only about 1800 square feet of space.

Sowing seeds, especially the tiny seeds of such flowers as cockscomb, larkspur, and ammobium, can be tedious. Many seed companies offer seed tapes, which, though more expensive, can make the job much easier. A wide variety of already-grown plants are available at nurseries to create an instant garden, but the choicest varieties—'Envy' zinnias and craspedia, for instance—are not available at garden centers.

It's my opinion that plants grown from seed sown directly in the ground are healthier in the long run. They avoid the suffering induced by transplant shock. Larkspur and cockscomb are just two of the many popular plants for drying that don't like to be moved. Try to sow seeds with a light hand in order to avoid having to transplant. If transplanting is necessary, move the plants into a water-soaked hole to prevent stress.

Place plants close together—not only to create glorious fields of color but also to discourage weed growth. To insure evenly sown or planted rows, stretch a cord tautly across the area before planting.

Over the years, I've grown many kinds of flowers, both new hybrids and old-time varieties, so I have a staple list of favorites. Each spring I add a few "experiments," secure in the knowledge that I can always rely on the following:

COCKSCOMB: The incredible cockscomb comes in two forms: feathery *(Celosia plumosa)* and crested *(C. cristata)*. The latter features fanlike blooms that resemble a rooster's crest—hence the plant's common name. I prefer this crested variety for its regal dried heads. 'Red Velvet' and pink 'Floradale' are two large-flowered beauties perfect for drying, whether used as whole blossoms or picked apart for smaller arrangements. Cockscomb does not transplant well, so when too many seeds produce a thick patch, gently pull out and discard the excess, leaving the correctly spaced plants undisturbed. It is best to soak the ground thoroughly before attempting this task.

GLOBE AMARANTH: Legend has it that Ben Franklin loved the cloverlike globe amaranth *(Gomphrena globosa)* and always had a fresh bouquet on his desk. Try some of the new varieties: 'Strawberry Fields' (orange/red) and 'Bicolor Rose' (soft lilac with white centers).

STRAWFLOWER: I buy strawflowers *(Helichrysum bracteatum)* in individual seed packets according to color, rather than in mixed packets, and for drying I especially favor the delightful cherry shades. Other optimum colors include silvery rose, canary yellow, pink, pure white, and the more recent 'Bikini', which supplies compact mounds of mixed colors.

SUNFLOWER: Sunflowers *(Helianthus annuus)*—fresh, dried, silk, or even screen-printed on curtains—have been the darlings of interior designers for some time, and new, low-growing varieties are very useful for drying. I'm especially fond of the 'Teddy Bear' sunflowers (available by mail order from seed companies, see page 201): These bushy, two- to three-foot-high plants provide armfuls of bright orange blossoms from three to five inches in diameter. They are truly distinctive.

ZINNIA: Dahlia-type, pastel-colored zinnias *(Zinnia elegans)* dry best. Other recommended varieties include 'Old Mexico', 'Candy Stripe', and 'Envy' (a luscious shade of lime-green that looks special fresh or dried). The improved, sturdy 'State Fair' and 'Tetra' zinnias are giant-flowered varieties that can be counted on for a continuous show of color.

DAHLIA: Dahlias *(Dahlia* hybrids*)* are half-hardy annuals, but they grow quickly and have a long flowering period, from late spring to late fall. Their tender bulbs won't survive cold winters in the ground, so they have to be dug up in autumn and stored in a frost-free location over winter. Tubers can be replanted the following spring. The showy, decorative type of dahlia dries best; the bedding and pompon dwarfs also dry exceptionally well; dried cactus-flowered dahlias, in my view, are less attractive.

OTHER ANNUALS well-suited for an "everlasting" collection include: larkspur *(Consolida ambigua)* and 'Green Pigmy' amaranthus—both excellent because of their spike-shaped blossoms; statice *(Limonium sinuatum)*, with its spectrum of long-lasting colors; acroclinium *(Helipterum roseum)*, with its dainty, daisylike flowers; bells of Ireland *(Moluccella laevis)*; blue salvia *(Salvia farinacea* 'Victoria'*)*; cornflowers *(Centaurea cyanus)*; immortelle *(Xeranthemum annuum)*; and winged everlasting *(Ammobium alatum)*.

GARDEN SHRUBS AND PERENNIALS

Perennials are a must for any cutting garden. Most are hardy and provide a dependable supply of blossoms for years. Although they can be grown from seed, as annuals are, it is often easier to buy plants from local nurseries. After a few years, you will probably have to divide the clumps, which will give you an opportunity to create new gardens for yourself—and for that new neighbor friend with the sunny yard.

BABY'S BREATH: I adore the cloudlike appearance of baby's breath *(Gypsophila paniculata)*, a hardy yet delicate-looking perennial. 'Bristol Fairy' and 'Perfecta', the best cultivars, can be propagated with stem cuttings in early summer.

DELPHINIUM: Shorter varieties of delphinium *(Delphinium elatum)*, such as 'Magic Fountains', are excellent for the average gardener (hummingbirds are quite fond of them, too). The numerous spikes are substantial in size and do not require staking. If you cut the flower stems to within a few inches of the ground after their initial spring blooming is over and fertilize the plants, you may force a second yield, although the stalks will be somewhat shorter. In my gardens, the delphinium 'Pacific Giant' reaches heights of over seven feet, and produces an array of spectacular colors that defies description.

HONESTY: If only for good luck, grow some honesty *(Lunaria annua* or *L. biennis)*, also known as money plant. It is slow to bloom, but once established will reseed itself for years. It is one of the few everlastings that prefers shade. Keeping some of its silvery, paperlike seedpods in a home is said to bring good luck to the occupants. I'm not superstitious, but I do tuck a few here and there throughout my house!

HYDRANGEA: Hydrangea bushes (*Hydrangea macrophylla*) are a must in every garden. They come in delicious shades of blue, pink, and green, and are wonderful additions to gardens in part-shade or even in sunny seaside locations. Their main requirement is lots of water. To maintain blue blossoms, plant in acid soil; for a pink hue, plant in alkaline soil. Lacecap hydrangeas don't dry as well as hortensia (snowball or "mop-head") types *(H. arborescens)*. Peegee hydrangeas *(H. paniculata* 'Grandiflora'*)*, with their huge, cone-shaped flower heads, can be hung to dry or dried in a desiccant.

LADY'S MANTLE: I added lady's mantle *(Alchemilla mollis)* to my perennial collection a few years ago, after seeing its beauty during a trip to England. With clusters of chartreuse flowers and large, handsome, silvery green leaves, it makes a wonderful ground cover in sun or shade. It also looks great spilling over the edge of a patio or walk.

PEONY: Peonies *(Paeonia* hybrids*)* belong in a class all their own. Second only to lilacs, they are my favorite spring flower to dry. Avoid planting peonies too deep or you will sacrifice blossoms. The older varieties, such as 'Sarah Bernhardt' and 'Festiva Maxima', tend to be the most fragrant. I also admire the Japanese single-flowered type, with its crested center. All varieties are very hardy, even where winters are extremely harsh.

ROSE: The rose *(Rosa* hybrids*)* is our country's national flower—and my personal favorite. All soft pastel shades of roses dry well, even the two-toned 'Heart's Delight'. Dark red roses, such as the long-stemmed beauties so popular on Valentine's Day, dry almost black. As a matter of fact, for a long time I thought it was impossible to achieve a bright red dried rose. By chance, I found the orange 'Tropicana' rose, which dries a clear Christmas-red. (This was a great relief when I wished to use some dried red roses in the White House for Nancy Reagan. I never did tell her that originally they were orange!)

Rose bushes require sun for at least six hours a day and love well-drained locations. I resist spraying my rose bushes, but I do give them monthly feedings of Ortho's Systemic Rose Food, which also seems to discourage most insect infestation. Recently, I discovered that miniature roses are tough survivors. They blossom profusely and make lovely border edgings for the hybrid tea roses. When dried for miniature nosegays and arrangements, they are absolutely precious.

Unfortunately, decades of hybridization, which have improved color and form, have eliminated fragrance from roses. As a result, intensely fragrant old roses, such as Bourbons and Albas, are making a comeback. My mother loved her rose garden, which included some wildly perfumed older varieties, such as 'Ramanas' rose. I am especially pleased with the David Austin cup-shaped English roses and with his 'Heritage' cultivar—both capture all the radiance of old roses. Another favorite is the carefree, pink 'The Fairy', so reminiscent of the old-fashioned 'Seven Sisters' variety my grandmother grew. 'The Fairy' is a hardy, disease-resistant plant with graceful clusters of pink rosettes literally covering the bush. Six of them were planted in the White House Rose Garden during the Bush Administration.

OTHER PERENNIALS perfect for drying include: coneflower *(Echinacea)*; foxglove *(Digitalis purpurea)*; German statice *(Goniolimon tataricum)*; globe thistle *(Echinops exaltatus)*; gloriosa daisy *(Rudbeckia hirta)*; hollyhock *(Alcea rosea)*; lavender *(Lavandula)*; liatris *(L. spicata)*; monkshood *(Aconitum napellus)*; pearly everlasting *(Anaphalis margaritacea)*; Shasta daisy *(Leucanthemum x superbum)*; yarrow *(Achillea)*— indispensable due to its straight, sturdy stems; Chinese lantern *(Physalis alkekengi)*; and 'Silver King' artemisia *(A. ludoviciana)*.

To my mind, 'Silver King' artemisia is a must in the dried flower field. Its silvery patina and long stems are essential to creating a strong outline for a design. A word of caution, however, regarding both 'Silver King' artemisia and Chinese lantern: Both have very invasive root systems that can smother a flower bed. I recommend placing these plants in separate areas to avoid the problem.

Some gardeners consider feverfew *(Tanacetum parthenium)* to be a nuisance, but I love its prolific, white, daisy-shaped heads. Once they appear in your garden, you'll have them forever. Cut the plant back after the first flush of bloom has ended, and you'll be rewarded with additional green foliage and more flowers later in the season.

CREATING AND CARING FOR A PRETTY GARDEN

Remember that dried flowers will be yours to view for many years, and grow your favorites. But experiment with different varieties. Each season I plant at least one new drying candidate, and every year I add many new flowers to my list of "musts"—although none has ever replaced my number one choice, the rose.

When planning your garden, don't make drying potential your only consideration. Intersperse some flowers you don't intend to dry among the others, so that the garden retains color and fullness while you're busy picking and cutting. Include begonias, cosmos, geraniums (the annual as well as the perennial types), impatiens, irises, lilies, petunias, phlox, spider flower, and morning glories, to name a few. They serve to fill a color void when harvesting time for drying purposes is at hand.

As a rule, I plant seeds at my farm over the Memorial Day weekend. There are two exceptions to the schedule: Larkspur, which germinates best in cool weather, is planted the month before; crested cockscomb, which doesn't like cool weather or soil, is planted a week or two after Memorial Day.

It used to be a bit of a secret that I talk to my flowers, just as my grandmother did many years ago. She would take me by the hand and walk me down the curved paths of her garden, all the while telling each variety to "perk up" because her granddaughter was coming to visit! Today, I follow her example and stroll hand-in-hand with my own granddaughter, talking to each floral specimen on the farm. Whether or not it really helps them grow, it's still a great form of therapy for the gardener.

All seeds and plants require nurturing to sprout and grow. Supply plenty of water (at least one inch each week) during dry periods, cultivate to aerate the soil and prevent weed growth, transplant when necessary, and remove spent blossoms to encourage new growth. Once a week, I prompt growth and an ample yield of flowers with an application of Miracle-Gro.®

Borders, such as a traditional white-picket fence or a hand-laid stone wall, serve to separate different gardens and insure evenly sown rows. Rose bushes grow along the fence posts, petunias and geraniums grace the stone wall, and the "spring" garden in the foreground features various perennials.

Chapter Two

GATHERING THE FLOWERS

What sunshine is to flowers,

smiles are to humanity.

JOSEPH ADDISON

THE RECENT RESURGENCE OF interest in gardening seems rooted in a desire to escape the hectic work world, even if that means getting a little dirt under the fingernails. The garden has become America's sanctuary. There's a certain satisfaction inherent in hands-on craft-making, but flower-drying is not a new phenomenon. Wreaths of dried acacia blossoms and garlands of larkspur covered the breast of the mummy of Ahmes I, ruler of ancient Egypt during the 22nd Dynasty (945–745 B.C.). In *The America of 1750*, author Peter Kalm notes that "naturally dried flowers decorated many homes." The colonists also included herbs for drying in their herb gardens, which were often conveniently located just outside the kitchen door. And Victorians developed flower-drying into an everyday art form. Today, unusual organic materials, whether from the open fields, the herb garden, the cutting garden, the florist's shop, or the street vendor, add to the originality of modern dried flower designs.

Flowers should be hung to dry in a warm, well-ventilated room. Gather flowers into groups of about seven stems, fasten with rubber bands, and hang upside down.

HERBS 🌿 Easily air-dried, the flower heads of oregano, clove, and onion make attractive additions to country-style arrangements and wildflower wreaths. I'm equally fond of the rich emerald green of curly parsley, which is best preserved in silica gel. It works fantastically as filler material, and is always a great conversation starter. If you grow oats, or have access to some, be sure to harvest them when still light green in color. Tied in bunches, they are a unique addition to a design.

STORE-BOUGHT CANDIDATES FOR DRYING 🌿 Supplementing a homegrown flower supply with purchases from a florist has never been more convenient. Bunches of flowers are available for sale not only at florist's shops but also on virtually every other street corner, and in supermarkets as well. An amateur hobbyist can purchase a variety of flowers and experiment.

It's important that store-bought flowers be fresh and not past their prime. Roses, for instance, can be tested by gently squeezing the buds. If they feel soft and spongy instead of firm, they are old stock or haven't been properly refrigerated—consequently, they won't dry well.

WILDFLOWERS 🌿 There are many wild field flowers that can be dried easily. Along roadsides and meadows, the possibilities are endless, but remember a few pointers before picking: Ask permission first from the landowner; identify the specific flower, to avoid inadvertently collecting a threatened or endangered species; and cut only a few stems from each stand, leaving a good-sized clump to go to seed.

Many field and forest plants can be hung to dry naturally and, once dried, won't reabsorb moisture from the air. For example, the spike form of dock, or sorrel, is a perfect wildflower to dry. Witness it in its spring green and rosy summer tones and, finally, in September's dark chocolate-brown. Chickweed makes a wonderful filler and wreath base (see THE SITTING DUCK, page 140). It is most attractive if picked when light green in color. White yarrow and pearly everlasting from the hillsides should be gathered early in the season—mid-August to early September—so that they will retain most of their pure white color when dried. Joe-Pye weed, with its dusty rose-pink flowers, is found in moist soil and must be gathered early, in the bud stage, or it will shatter when dried. Purple lythrum and golden yellow tansy are also popular additions to informal dried arrangements. Lythrum is a very invasive, non-native plant that should not be cultivated in a garden, only picked in the wild. Goldenrod and cattails should also be picked early in the season. After air-drying, goldenrod should be sprayed with several coats of clear acrylic sealer or hair spray. Cattails, when dry, should be dipped in shellac to prevent shedding. Bittersweet vines can be found along roadsides, and are very useful for fall creations (see BITTERSWEET HALLOWEEN

WREATH, page 176). Pick the bittersweet early, just as the berries start to show their orange color. (Note: This vine is listed as endangered in many states—it's being crowded out by its Asian cousin.) The delicate Queen Anne's lace can also be hung to dry, but it is so much more attractive when processed in a drying desiccant, such as silica gel.

Wildflowers lend themselves to country-style arrangements, but I also occasionally use them in combination with garden varieties—for example, wild brown dock with garden-grown yellow yarrow and black-eyed Susan. For more formal dried designs, though, only garden flowers will do.

PICKING FLOWERS One of the hardest things for beginners to do is pluck any of their lavish bounty. Most gardeners procrastinate, reluctant to behead their precious beauties. But come fall and winter, when the garden is bare and nothing remains to remind you of summer's glory, such hesitation will have been in vain. So force yourself. This does not mean indiscriminately scalping beds of blossoms, however. A few here and there will not be missed. Discretion is the better part of valor!

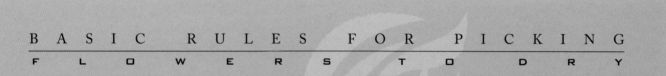

BASIC RULES FOR PICKING FLOWERS TO DRY

- Cut stems at bouquet-length, using clippers or very sharp scissors.

- Cut specimens by midday, before the hot summer sun has a chance to wilt them.

- Avoid picking right after a storm or in the early morning hours, when blossoms are wet with rain or dew. If you must pick a particular rain-soaked blossom, place it indoors in a vase filled with water so the petals can dry but the flower won't wilt.

- Choose only the most perfect specimens as candidates for drying: A miserable fresh blossom is a miserable dried blossom.

- Most flowers should be picked just at their peak, when they're brimming with brilliant color and sturdy form.

- If you cannot begin the drying process immediately after picking the flowers, put them in a vase of cool water and place in a dark location.

- Cut bud formations in addition to blossoms for more realistic dried designs.

FRESH AND DRIED

The pleasing, rounded forms of whole fruits and vegetables add an element of surprise to traditional floral designs—all it takes is an old mason jar, some fresh asparagus spears, and a few pussy willow branches to create this innovative arrangement.

Materials

1-quart mason jar

1 block florist's foam, soaked
    in water

1 large, wide rubber band

1½ yards white wired-ribbon

30 large asparagus spears, fresh

7 acacia stems, fresh

9 Boston fern fronds, fresh

3 silver-dollar eucalyptus
    branches, fresh

3 yellow lily stems, fresh

6 irises, fresh

5 pussy willow branches,
    air-dried

Instructions

1. Fill mason jar with wet florist's foam.

2. Place rubber band around middle of jar. Insert asparagus spears, tips up, under rubber band, all around jar.

3. Insert acacia stems, fern fronds, and eucalyptus branches into florist's foam, to create height at the back of the design.

4. Position lily stems in a triangular pattern in the center of the arrangement.

5. Add 3 or 4 irises at an angle, so that they hang below the rim of the jar, and scatter the rest among the lilies, graduating the stems' lengths so that they reach to the top of the arrangement.

6. Insert pussy willow branches as accents.

7. Wrap ribbon around jar to conceal rubber band, and tie in a bow.

GLOBE AMARANTH HEART

Globe amaranth, a bushy, bedding annual originally from Southeast Asia, is prized for its papery, pomponlike blossoms. Colors range from pink and purple to yellow, orange, and white. This heart-shaped wreath, trimmed in lace, tied with satin, and garnished with baby's breath, makes an unabashedly feminine statement.

Materials

6-inch-wide Styrofoam
heart form

19-gauge florist's wire

Hot-glue gun with clear
glue sticks

2 yards two-inch-deep blue
ruffled lace

1 yard ¼-inch-wide pink
satin ribbon

Bits of baby's breath, air-dried

16 pink globe amaranth,
air-dried

4 stems white ammobium,
air-dried

Instructions

1. Using hot-glue gun, attach lace along back of wreath, so that ruffles frame form.
2. To make a loop for hanging, cut a section of 19-gauge florist's wire, twist ends together, and insert ends into top of Styrofoam form.
3. Tie a long, multi-looped bow from satin ribbon and glue to front of heart (refer to photo for placement).
4. Glue bits of baby's breath all around wreath's surface.
5. Position globe amaranth all around wreath's surface, following outline of heart and couching blossoms in baby's breath; then glue individual flowers into place.
6. Glue touches of ammobium to top and bottom of wreath.

part two

TIME TO DRY

Chapter Three

HANGING TO DRY

*Beauty is the only thing
which time cannot harm.*

OSCAR WILDE

THE MOST COMMONLY USED AND easiest method of preserving flowers is air-drying. Flowers dried using this method usually supply the outline or backbone of designs that incorporate focal flowers dried in a desiccant such as silica gel (lilacs, marigolds, peonies, roses, zinnias, and the like). Some of these air-dried everlastings are spiky in form: annual and perennial statice, amaranthus, delphinium, heather, larkspur, liatris, and lamb's-ears. Some are airy, such as baby's breath and lady's mantle. Others, like celosia and yarrow, are full or bulky; and still others are wonderfully small or daisylike—ammobium, globe amaranth, and strawflowers.

Flowers picked to be air-dried should be as perfect as possible and moisture-free. Unlike flowers for fresh use, those chosen for drying should not be picked too early in the day. Let the warmth of the sun evaporate the dew first, and remove leaves from the stems to facilitate rapid drying. The faster flowers dry, the better they retain their colors.

Most flowers air-dry best when hung upside down, but some, such as dock, pussy willow, and goldenrod, dry with more graceful curves if set upright in containers.

FINDING A SPACE ✿ Suitable places for drying flowers include warm, dry rooms in which there is some air movement. Attics, barns, spare rooms, or garages are all fine, but never use basements—they tend to be too damp. While most air-dried flowers defy any humidity damage, some may develop mold. If you are really desperate for drying space, take another look at a bedroom closet or, better yet, the guestroom closet. Push some of the clothes to one side, and there will be just enough room for a few coat hangers on which to suspend air-drying flowers.

Drying racks can be used where space is at a premium. Freestanding "accordion-style" racks are available in department stores, and antique shops occasionally offer the wonderful old-fashioned ones that hang from the wall and extend adjustable wooden dowels. At our farm, my husband suspended bamboo poles and screw hooks (the type used to hang teacups) from the beams of the kitchen ceiling. The rubber bands used to hold the flower stems together slip on and off the hooks easily.

Dried materials can remain hanging indefinitely, as long as they are not subjected to extreme dampness. A dehumidifier is a great asset in a room where dampness is a severe problem. To store the flowers after they're dry, place them between layers of tissue paper in cardboard boxes.

Below, the regal crested cockscomb, which dries a deep red. To the right, pretty little button zinnias, which make colorful fillers in large dried designs.

THE BASICS OF AIR-DRYING ✤ Most flowers air-dry best when hung upside down, but some plants, such as dock, pussy willow, goldenrod, and many grasses, dry with more graceful curves if they're set upright—in a vase, for instance. When hanging to dry, gather flowers into bunches of seven or eight stems, fasten with rubber bands, and hang upside down. If drying large quantities of a particular variety, separate the bunches according to color. As the stems dry and shrink, the rubber bands will contract and keep the bunches together—something that string or wire cannot accomplish.

ANNUALS FOR AIR-DRYING

ACROCLINIUM: *Helipterum roseum* has daisylike flowers that range in color from white and pink to shades of red, usually with black centers. They hold their color well when dried and are attractive used individually or in bunches.

When to pick: Harvest before flowers are fully open; they develop further while drying.

How to dry: Acroclinium can be hung to dry on its own stems, or it can be wired prior to drying. Wired stems allow for more flexibility when arranging. For instructions on how to wire acroclinium, see the strawflower listing below or the FLOWER-DRYING PANTRY on page 200.

Time to dry: Stand upright in a container for two to three weeks.

AGERATUM: Small and dainty, blue ageratum *(Ageratum houstonianum)* is great for air-drying. The white form tends to turn muddy when dried.

When to pick: Pick as soon as the individual flower heads open.

How to dry: Using a small rubber band, gather three to four heads together. The short stems will usually require wiring (see page 200). If you are pressed for time at the end of the season when a frost is due, you can pull up the entire plant and hang it to dry.

Time to dry: Ageratum dries in three weeks.

BELLS OF IRELAND: Although bells of Ireland *(Moluccella laevis)* can be air-dried, to best retain the green color, process with a desiccant or with glycerine: These methods are explained in Chapters 4 and 6, respectively.

When to pick: Cut when bells are firm to the touch and before lower bells begin to fade.

How to dry: Before drying, remove the leaves carefully with small, sharp scissors, then hang stems upside down individually. After flowers have dried, dab a drop of white craft glue where the shell-like calyxes join the stem, because otherwise they tend to fall off.

Time to dry: Bells of Ireland will dry within three weeks.

COCKSCOMB: A very classy flower, the crested cockscomb *(Celosia cristata)* adds a regal finishing touch to any arrangement. It is especially appropriate in Victorian designs. 'Red Velvet' and pink 'Floradale' are my two favorites, but I still plant an unnamed variety grown by my grandmother, who passed the seeds on to my mother. She gave them to me and I have given some to my own two daughters. What a great heritage to share!

When to pick: Cut stems just before flowers are in full bloom, usually in late summer, and definitely before the first fall frost.

How to dry: This glorious flower requires a little extra care to dry, but it is well worth the effort. Many observers have remarked that my dried cockscomb are especially vibrant in color and velvety in texture. I attribute this to the following method: Hang individual stems upside down, taped onto coat hangers, with an open paper bag pulled up over each flower head and taped to the sides of the hanger. Tiny seeds will fall into the bag, and flower color will intensify. After removing the dried cockscomb, gently scrape off any loose seeds from the flower heads so they won't drop after arranging. To maintain its velvety texture, never spray the dried cockscomb; it will become matted and dull. Large dried heads can be divided into smaller sections for use as accents.

Time to dry: Allow at least three weeks for the heads to dry.

CRASPEDIA: An annual in the Northeast, craspedia *(Craspedia globosa)* is a perennial in warmer climates (below Zone 8). Its bright yellow, globe-shaped flowers and long, sturdy stems make it the perfect accent in small designs, and, grouped in larger bunches, a strong focal point in more lavish arrangements.

When to pick: Cut long stems when the flowers have just fully opened.

How to dry: Hang upside down in small bunches so that the long stems dry straight.

Time to dry: Hang for three weeks.

GLOBE AMARANTH: The lovely colors of this cloverlike everlasting are wonderful: lavender, white, pink, orange, and the new 'Bicolor Rose' variety. The dwarf cultivar 'Buddy' is also charming. Globe amaranth *(Gomphrena globosa)* has sturdy stems and is useful in small designs. Clustered together into groups of five or six stems, they combine well with larger flowers.

When to pick: To retain color, cut when flowers are fully open.

How to dry: To prevent tangling, hang in bunches that are well separated. At season's end, you can pull up entire globe amaranth plants and hang them to dry.

Time to dry: Dries quickly, in one to two weeks, but should be left hanging for at least three weeks so that the stems become firm.

LARKSPUR: *Consolida ambigua* keeps its color well when dried and is one of the most popular flowers for creating the outline of an arrangement.

When to pick: As long as the tips of the flower spike are still tightly closed along at least one inch of the stem, larkspur can be air-dried. If the whole spike is open, the flowers will drop off while drying.

How to dry: Gather and bundle larkspur according to color, since at least six to eight stems of each color are usually used in a design.

Time to dry: Larkspur dries in three weeks.

STATICE: All forms of statice dry well, but I'm particularly impressed with the mauve shade of rattail, or Russian, statice *(Psylliostachys suworowii)*. Although its growth habit is rather lanky compared to bushy annual statice *(Limonium sinuatum)* and perennial, or German, statice *(Goniolimon tataricum),* its delicate form and color always create interest in dried arrangements. All statice make great fillers.

When to pick: Statice should be picked as soon as the florets open and show color.

How to dry: Bunch loosely, by color, to make it easier to use them in arrangments.

Time to dry: Generally three weeks, but Russian statice takes two weeks and German statice, one week.

STRAWFLOWER: Many gardeners simply pick their strawflowers *(Helichrysum bracteatum)* and hang them to dry on their own stems. I prefer to wire the stems, using the method described below. Strawflowers dried this way are more versatile. They can be inserted into fresh as well as dried arrangements, since there are no stems to rot.

When to pick: Pick strawflowers when they are still in the bud stage. Cut the heads off the stems. Carefully insert lengths of 19- or 20-gauge florist's wire into the base of the bud, where the stem has been cut off, just deep enough to penetrate.

How to dry: Place the individually wired strawflowers upright in a container.

Time to dry: Within two weeks the buds will open and—magically, it seems—secure themselves to the wire.

XERANTHEMUM: These daisylike flowers *(Xeranthemum annuum)* have stiff petals that are naturally strawlike. They come in soft shades of white, lilac, dusty pink, and rosy pink. Use them individually in dainty designs or massed in bunches for larger arrangements.

When to pick: Cut single stems as soon as flowers are fully open. Cut some stems in bud.

How to dry: Gather in small bunches of four to five stems and hang upside down.

Time to dry: Open flowers will dry in two weeks. Buds take three weeks.

ARTEMISIA: There are many types of artemisia, or wormwood *(Artemisia ludoviciana)*. My favorite perennial variety is 'Silver King' because its silvery gray stems air-dry rapidly and make great material for the outline of a design.

When to pick: Pick 'Silver King' artemisia while the tiny flowers still retain their silvery patina. If you wait, the flower heads may turn an unappealing brownish color.

How to dry: Cut stems as long as possible and bunch six to eight stems together to hang upside down. The best way to fashion a wreath with artemisia is to do so while it's fresh and pliable. Using thin spool-wire, attach bunches of stems to a circular wire or Styrofoam form; then lay the wreath flat to dry. Once the artemisia has dried, some of the wire wrapping can be removed. The intertwined pieces will have dried and hardened in position.

Time to dry: Leave hanging upside down for at least three weeks to be sure stems have hardened. If wrapped around a wreath form, allow three to four weeks.

ASTILBE: Sometimes called false goatsbeard, astilbe *(Astilbe biternata* or *A. davidii)* is noted for its plumes of pink, lavender, white, or dark red flowers. All but the whites can be air-dried; white varieties discolor unless they are dried in a desiccant.

When to pick: Cut stems as soon as flowers are fully open but before they reach maturity.

How to dry: Hang bunches of three to four stems upside down.

Time to dry: Three weeks.

CHINESE LANTERN: With their leaves removed, bunches of Chinese lantern *(Physalis alkekengi)* make colorful additions to designs and last indefinitely if kept out of direct sunlight.

When to pick: Pick when most of the lanterns on the stems are orange, but definitely before the first frost.

How to dry: These dry easily when hung upside down in bunches or placed upright in an arrangement. After they are dried, you can turn the lantern-shaped flowers into open, full-faced flowers: Using a pair of small pointed scissors, start at the slender tip and cut through every other vein; gently coax back the individual, newly formed "petals" to expose the berrylike ball in the center. Just a few of these opened "flowers" add interest to a rather ordinary branch. (See RUSTIC FALL ARRANGEMENT, page 127).

Time to dry: Whether hanging upside down or standing in an arrangement, Chinese lantern dries in two to three weeks.

DELPHINIUM: Closely associated with larkspur, delphinium *(Delphinium elatum)* are majestic flowers that retain their color for years once dried. Unlike larkspur, delphinium are perennial, so they don't have to be replanted each year.

When to pick: As long as the tips of the flower spike are still tightly closed along at least one inch of the stem, delphinium can be air-dried. If the whole spike is open, the flowers will drop off while drying.

How to dry: Hang individually rather than in bunches.

Time to dry: Delphinium dry in three weeks.

GLOBE THISTLE: These steel-blue, globe-shaped flowers *(Echinops exaltatus)* are very useful additions to dried designs.

When to pick: Cut the stems precisely when the green heads start to show a slight blue color; fully flowered heads will turn brownish and fall apart. Wear garden gloves when picking, as the prickly gray leaves can be quite irritating.

How to dry: Hang bundles of six to seven stems upside down.

Time to dry: Globe thistle dries in three weeks; handle carefully when dry to avoid breaking off the flowers.

HEATHER: The rosy shades of heather *(Calluna vulgaris)* dry best.

When to pick: Cut branches before the flowers are completely open.

How to dry: Hang branches in bunches. Spray with a fixative, such as hair spray, when dry.

Time to dry: Heather dries rapidly, usually in two weeks.

LADY'S MANTLE: An excellent, gold-toned filler in the garden and in arrangements, lady's mantle *(Alchemilla mollis)* dries perfectly and easily. The airy flower clusters are a real delight, and hold their yellow color year after year.

When to pick: Cut as soon as the flowers are fully open and still slightly green. Cut the stems as long as possible because they harden while air-drying and facilitate arranging.

How to dry: Hang flower stems, with or without leaves, upside down, individually or in small bunches.

Time to dry: Stems without leaves dry quickly, usually in one week; stems with leaves take about three weeks.

LAVENDER: A real standout for color as well as fragrance, lavender *(Lavandula)* is available in a range of colors, from deep purples to frosty blues.

When to pick: It's imperative to pick lavender before the flowers open along the stem (they open from the top down). Be sure to include some leaves—they emit an amazingly strong perfume. To prolong the blooming period of the plant, pick frequently. A handful of dried lavender tied with a pretty pastel ribbon makes a lovely accent for the bedroom (see LACE FAN AND LAVENDER BUNCH, page 96).

How to dry: With lavender, as with artemisia, if you want to make a wreath, do so while the stems are fresh and pliable, then lay the wreath flat to dry. Otherwise, tie stems together in a bunch, secure with a rubber band (disguised with a ribbon if you wish), and hang to dry in a closet—or on a wall where it can be enjoyed while it's drying.

Time to dry: Lavender dries quickly, usually within two weeks.

LIATRIS: Also known as gay feather, liatris *(Liatris spicata)* has bright lavender or purple spikes. Its strong color combines beautifully with gray artemisia and lamb's-ears.

When to pick: Cut a stem when half the blossoms on its spike are fully open. Unlike most spiky flowers, liatris bears buds that open from the top downward.

How to dry: Liatris can be dried upright or hanging in bunches of six to seven stems.

Time to dry: Upright or hanging, liatris takes about three weeks to dry.

PEARLY EVERLASTING: Because a clear, as opposed to creamy, white is hard to achieve in dried flowers, I dry large quantities of perennial pearly everlasting *(Anaphalis margaritacea),* as well as annual ammobium and strawflower. All three make splendid white filler flowers.

When to pick: This is another flower cluster that should be collected in the bud stage. If the flowers are open, they will shatter while drying.

How to dry: Bunch the tightly budded heads in groups of seven to eight stems and hang upside down.

Time to dry: Flowers are usually dried and stems hardened in three weeks.

YARROW: A sturdy, popular, and easy-to-dry perennial, yarrow *(Achillea)* has large, flat heads of distinctive yellow flowers that emit a pungent fragrance. It is a rugged plant that blooms from June through September. There are many types of yarrow, but I prefer *A. filipendulina* for drying. Avoid the dwarf white *A. ptarmica* 'The Pearl' because its flower structure is too tiny.

When to pick: Flat flower clusters should be gathered while still bright yellow. Blossoms mature rapidly, so check plants daily.

How to dry: To keep the dried florets' pollen from dropping, spritz the heads before and after drying with a clear acrylic spray or an extra-hold hair spray. Gather the stems into small bunches, staggering the flowers to avoid damaging the shape of each head. For a more open flower head, dry stems upright in a vase. Pastel yarrows (*A. millefolium* 'Cerise Queen' and 'Summer Pastels') retain their colors best if processed in silica gel. *Time to dry:* Three weeks.

SHRUBS, VINES, AND GRASSES FOR AIR-DRYING

ACACIA: Also known as mimosa, acacia *(Acacia)* is a shrublike tree with clusters of small, yellow, round flowers and fernlike, light green leaves. It creates a wonderful cascading effect in arrangements, and is quick to dry.

When to pick: Cut stems when in full flower, keeping the leaves on the stems (they air-dry attractively).

How to dry: Hang upside down in bunches of two or three stems.

Time to dry: About three weeks.

BITTERSWEET: I grow my own bittersweet *(Celastrus scandens)* vines, which are readily available from mail-order catalogs (although in some areas *C. orbiculatus,* Asian bittersweet, is considered a nuisance weed). One plant alone will not produce berries: At least two plants are necessary. Use the dried vines in fall and winter for holiday arrangements and accents.

When to pick: Clip stems early, just as the orange color is starting to show on the berry clusters, or the orange fruit will open too quickly and shatter. The unripe berries will open in 7 to 10 days, actually brighten in color, and retain their form when used.

How to dry: Before drying, while branches are still pliable, you can fashion airy wreaths from excess bittersweet vines for wall or door decorations. To dry, hang bunches of the berried vine upside down. Keep or remove the leaves from the vines as you wish.

Time to dry: Bittersweet dries rapidly, usually in two weeks.

GRASSES: There are many grasses, both ornamental and edible, with interesting flower heads for air-drying. I'm particularly fond of beard grass *(Polypogon monspeliensis),* oat grass *(Avena sativa),* pampas grass *(Cortaderia selloana),* wheat *(Triticum aestivum),* and sweet corn *(Zea mays).* I harvest oats when they still have a soft green coloring, which complements spring and fall arrangements and supplies a green accent so necessary in dried creations. Picked before the heads become too fluffy, pampas grass can be placed upright to air-dry naturally in fall arrangements.

When to pick: Pick grasses as soon as flower heads have fully opened.

How to dry: Hang upside down in bunches of six or seven stems, depending on thickness.

Time to dry: Allow a minimum of three weeks to harden off stems.

HOP VINE: One of my favorite vines for air-drying is the hop vine *(Humulus lupulus)*. A neighbor introduced me to this prolific plant by giving me a small shoot from her garden. Although it's no longer popular for beer-making in upstate New York, it has taken on a new identity in the flower world because of its unique pale green flower clusters. Green is a precious color in dried creations: The introduction of any green material creates a more realistic design. Hop flowers are a great conversation piece, too. They can rarely be identified by the average gardener or flower lover.

When to pick: Hops are rapidly growing perennial vines that withstand drastic cuttings of various lengths, all of which dry and become graceful additions to arrangements or wreaths (see BERIBBONED STRAWFLOWER WREATH, page 124). Cut flower clusters or lengths of vine when they are still a soft green.

How to dry: Strip leaves off stems to speed drying. Hang upside down in bunches.

Time to dry: Depending on the length of the vine, two to three weeks.

HYDRANGEA, PEEGEE: One of the most popular hang-to-dry flowers for novices, Peegee hydrangea *(Hydrangea paniculata* 'Grandiflora') is as prominent today as it was in Victorian times. Grown as a shrub or small tree, Peegee hydrangea can reach 10 feet in height and is hardy in Zones 3 to 8. For larger flower heads, prune out a number of the shrub's center stems and be sure to water during dry periods. The large dried heads can be broken apart into smaller clusters for use in a range of designs.

When to pick: For added beauty, try cutting the branches when the showy heads are still tinged with rosy pink hues instead of dull tones of golden brown evident later.

How to dry: Hang the flowers of Peegee hydrangea in bunches, or arrange them in their fresh state and let dry in place.

Time to dry: Hydrangeas dry rapidly, in one to two weeks.

HYDRANGEA, WHITE (SNOWBALL): White hydrangeas *(H. arborescens)* are gems that air-dry beautifully. (Blue, pink, and purple hydrangeas are best dried in a desiccant.)

When to pick: As soon as the white flowers turn a soft lime green, pick the stems. This shade of green is very useful in dried creations, and at this stage the flower retains its shape after drying. If you wait too long to pick them, the blossoms will become speckled with brown.

How to dry: Remove the leaves and hang the stems upside down in small bunches.

Time to dry: One to two weeks is sufficient.

PUSSY WILLOW: Pussy willows *(Salix discolor)* are always a welcome sign of spring. A bunch of pussy willow stems, contained with rubber bands, tied with a raffia bow, and hung upside down, makes an impressive decoration for the front door.

When to pick: Cut stems in the early stages of flowering, when the tips are just starting to open and before they get a "fluffy" appearance.

How to dry: For special effects, tape or wire the stems of pussy willows, while they're fresh and supple, into spiral or curved shapes; then air-dry them in an upright position. The tape or wire can be removed after drying. Bunches of stems may also be dried standing upright in a vase or hanging upside down.

Time to dry: It takes about three weeks for the flowers to dry.

FLOWERS THAT HANG TO DRY

ACACIA	COCKSCOMB	LAMB'S-EARS
ACROCLINIUM	CRASPEDIA	LARKSPUR
AMARANTHUS	DELPHINIUM	LAVENDER
AMMOBIUM	DOCK	LIATRIS
ARTEMISIA	GLOBE AMARANTH	PEARLY EVERLASTING
ASTILBE	GLOBE THISTLE	PUSSY WILLOW
BABY'S BREATH	GOLDENROD	STARFLOWER
BACHELOR'S BUTTON	GRASSES	STATICE
BELLS OF IRELAND	HEATHER	STRAWFLOWER
BITTERSWEET	HOP VINE	TANSY
BLUE AGERATUM	HYDRANGEA	XERANTHEMUM
CHINESE LANTERN	LADY'S MANTLE	YARROW

DELIGHTFUL WICKER BASKET

All of the flowers in this basket, which is sitting on a wicker table in the gazebo at my farm, are air-dried. Air-dried flowers are much more desirable for outdoor displays because they tolerate the elements better than do desiccant-dried flowers. The method for this arrangement is easy, and the results charming. Remember to wire strawflowers prior to drying them.

Materials

Wicker basket with handle, about 9 inches wide at base	10 blue larkspur
2 blocks florist's foam	24 dark pink heather
1½ yards three-inch-wide floral ribbon	3 pink crested cockscomb
1 long wired pick	20 bunches of statice (3 stems per bunch), assorted pink and lavender
19-gauge florist's wire	6 bunches white pearly everlasting (3 stems per bunch)
22 'Silver King' artemisia	
7 pale blue delphinium	12 pink strawflowers
10 white larkspur	12 white strawflowers
10 pink larkspur	8 blue globe thistle

Instructions

1. Wedge florist's foam into basket.
2. Insert spiky materials to form the outer dimensions of the arrangement—artemisia first, followed by delphinium and then larkspur.
3. Insert heather so that some of it spills out over the basket.
4. Add 2 cockscomb to the right and left near the handle, just above the basket rim, and position the third so that it reaches halfway up the handle.
5. Using florist's wire, tie bunches of statice, and insert throughout arrangement.
6. Tie the ribbon into a bow with long streamers and wire it to the pick. Insert pick in florist's foam at the very base of the basket handle.
7. Scatter pearly everlasting bunches, strawflowers, and globe thistle wherever there are empty spaces, placing some through the loops of the bow.

DRIED, WITH A TOUCH OF SILK

According to Victorian tradition, 'Silver King' artemisia represents remembrance, larkspur signifies devotion, and globe amaranth, immortality. This pretty combination of air-dried and silk flowers could last an eternity—just be sure that the silk flowers look realistic.

Materials

DRIED FLOWERS:

10 'Silver King' artemisia

5 pink Russian statice

6 pink larkspur

6 purple larkspur

2 burgundy crested cockscomb

30 bicolor globe amaranth

14 strawflowers, mostly white, a few pink

5 blue globe thistle

SILK FLOWERS:

6 blue cornflowers

4 pink cosmos

3 ivy or other green-leaf stems

Dark cobalt-blue pitcher

1 block florist's foam

19-gauge florist's wire

Green floral tape

Instructions

1. Secure florist's foam in pitcher, leaving 2 inches extended above the rim.
2. Define outer dimensions of the arrangement with 'Silver King' artemisia, Russian statice, and larkspur.
3. Place cockscomb as focal points near the center-base of the design.
4. Gather globe amaranth into clusters of 3 to 4 stems each, wire and tape each cluster, and insert at outer edges of the arrangement. (For instructions on how to wire flowers, see page 200.)
5. Scatter strawflowers wherever lighter colors are needed.
6. Insert blue cornflowers deep within the design, as background for the bright pink cosmos, which are placed above and to the right and left of the cockscomb.
7. Add the ivy stems as accents, at the bottom and back of the design.
8. Place globe thistle last (as they break easily).
9. Set a separate bunch of globe amaranth at the base of the arrangement.

Chapter Four

DRYING WITH
DESICCANTS

Plant a seed of friendship;

Reap a bouquet of happiness.

LOIS L. KAUFMAN

FOR STUNNING RESULTS WHEN drying distinctive, dramatically shaped flowers such as dahlias, lilacs, marigolds, peonies, roses, snapdragons, and zinnias, it's best to work with a drying agent, or desiccant. Using a desiccant, such as silica gel, requires some patience, but the high-quality results more than make up for the extra effort.

I have tried many other drying agents besides silica gel, including borax, borax with cornmeal, sand, and even cat litter. Sand would probably take second place to silica gel, but it has the disadvantages of a prolonged drying time (up to three weeks) and a heavy weight (which is potentially damaging to the flowers).

Although there are many silica-gel-based products available at craft and floral supply stores, I recommend Flower-Dri.® It is a finely powdered, sugarlike substance containing blue granules that lose their color when the material is saturated with moisture. Usually, Flower-Dri® can be used three to four times before it

When drying with desiccants, most blossoms are placed face-up in a one-inch-deep layer of silica gel or other processing agent.

has to be restored—an easy process in itself. Simply heat the desiccant, uncovered, in a 250-degree oven, stirring occasionally, for about one hour. To avoid damaging your flowers, be sure to allow the silica gel to cool completely before re-use. Although it is initially more expensive than some other products, Flower-Dri® silica gel has lasting qualities and can be used over and over—for as long as 15 years.

Air-drying is a relatively slow process, but desiccants absorb moisture from a flower with great rapidity, thereby helping it to retain its shape and color. In most cases, desiccant-dried garden flowers are practically indistinguishable from fresh. Due to the rapid drying time afforded by silica gel and the introduction of the microwave as a tool for flower-drying (see Chapter 5), however, other desiccants may ultimately become obsolete in the field.

CONTAINERS FOR DESICCANT-DRYING Empty cookie and fruitcake tins and coffee cans with tight-fitting lids make excellent containers when drying with silica gel. For the truly devoted dried-flower enthusiast, large, rectangular, disposable aluminum pans covered with heavy-duty foil allow for more space to dry. (On seeing such pans throughout various rooms of my house, visitors have often remarked, "But when do you find the time to bake all this lasagne?") When using a desiccant other than silica gel, an uncovered shoe box will do.

DRYING WITH SILICA GEL To begin, fill an empty tin with an even layer of silica gel, one inch deep. Cut off all but one inch of the flower's stem. If drying double- or many-petaled flowers, place them face-up in the silica gel. Place single-petaled blossoms, such as daisies, face-down on top of the silica gel base. Flowers that have long stalks, such as bells of Ireland and snapdragons, should be laid lengthwise in the container. To dry tulips, place each bloom face-up in a paper cup containing one inch of silica gel; this way, the sides and center of the tulip are much more easily filled with granules, and the shape of the flower is better preserved. And always include some buds in your drying collection, especially buds of roses and peonies, because they add realistic charm to everlasting creations. Cut the buds with one-inch stems and lay them horizontally in the silica gel.

Gently cover the blossom, using a small spoon to dust the gel over it, starting from the outer edges and working toward the center until the specimen is completely covered. Work slowly and carefully, as the flower will dry in the shape in which it is covered. It is important to dust the desiccant crystals between the petals—of a rose, for instance—or within the cupped shapes of multipetaled flowers—such as peonies—without distorting the petals' shape and position. Buds may require a few extra days to dry because their tight centers are impervious to the drying desiccant.

It is a sensible idea to place like varieties of flowers in the same container. Different varieties can be included in one container provided that their drying times are similar. Refer to the FLOWER-DRYING CHART on page 80 to compare drying times for specific flowers.

Cover the container with its lid or with a sheet of aluminum foil taped in place. Label each container with the contents and date, for future reference. The container can be stored on a closet shelf or, if space is a problem, underneath a bed.

Most flowers should not be left in silica gel longer than seven days if they are to retain their color, shape, and flexibility for wiring and arranging. Plant material dried with a desiccant tends to become brittle if left too long in the agent. Silica gel in particular produces heat: Flowers will burn if buried in an airtight container. For this reason, it is imperative to follow the guidelines listed in the FLOWER-DRYING CHART on page 80.

When the drying time has expired, the specimens should feel crisp and taffeta-like to the touch. If they are limp, replace the cover and leave them for another day or two. If the flowers fail to dry properly, discard them and try again with another specimen, after considering and correcting the possible problem. The flowers may have been wet from dew or rain before processing, the drying agent may have required reheating to restore its absorption qualities, or the cover may not have been airtight. If the flower was succulent by nature, it was not a good choice for drying.

After slowly pouring off some of the desiccant and scooping an open hand under the specimen, lift the flower out, turn it upside down, and give it a light tap or shake. Any powdery residue can be removed with a small camel's-hair brush. Next, insert the stem into a one-inch-thick slice of florist's foam. This is an ideal way to store dried materials. Upright, they retain their shape and are protected from being crushed or distorted. Place the foam in a storage box—a plastic or cardboard dress, sweater, or coat box is a good size. Use a box with a secure lid so the flowers don't get dusty or damp. Empty cardboard egg cartons are ideal for holding dried roses, one to a cup.

FLOWERS FOR
DESICCANT-DRYING

BELLS OF IRELAND

CHIVES IN BLOOM

DAHLIA

DAISY

DELPHINIUM

DOGWOOD

FEVERFEW

LILAC

LILY-OF-THE-VALLEY

MARIGOLD

OREGANO IN BLOOM

PARSLEY

PEONY, FLOWER AND BUD

ROSE, FLOWER AND BUD

SNAPDRAGON

ZINNIA

I have never had a bug problem in storage, but have heard stories from other enthusiasts. Apparently, dried peonies and strawflowers are often the culprits. As a preventive measure against such problems, put a few mothballs in the storage box.

To ward off any damage from humidity, place a few tablespoons of desiccant in the storage box until the flowers are removed and arranged. Once the flowers are on display, during the winter months, home heating will keep them dry. If an area is particularly damp and the arrangements warrant special protection, apply several light coats of clear matte acrylic spray, flower sealer, or hair spray. As long as they are in an air-conditioned environment during the summer months, dried flower arrangements need no further protection.

DRYING WITH OTHER DESICCANTS ❧ Keep in mind the following attributes of drying agents other than silica gel:

- ❧ Borax and borax with cornmeal sometimes give finished flowers an undesirable, waxlike coating.
- ❧ Cornmeal added to borax helps flowers retain color; borax helps prevent possible weevil damage from cornmeal.
- ❧ If borax becomes lumpy, it should be sifted before use.
- ❧ Any sand other than the sterilized play sand used in children's sandboxes must be washed thoroughly prior to processing.

All of the above drying agents should be poured to a level depth of two to three inches in the bottom of a shoe box. Place flowers face-up or -down, according to the guidelines listed in the preceding silica-drying section, before covering completely with the agent. It is not necessary to cover the box with a lid or with foil. Label each box for reference, listing its contents on a piece of paper affixed to a corner of the box.

Drying times vary from ten days to three weeks. Flowers may be left in the open box for long periods without incurring any damage. Unlike silica gel, desiccants such as borax, borax with cornmeal, and sand do not produce heat, and so timing is not as crucial.

Most flowers must be dusted with a brush when dry to remove coatings and powdery deposits left by the desiccant. The resulting colors will never be as vivid as those achieved through silica gel processing, although some results with sand are quite good.

COLOR CHANGES ❧ The color of a flower changes in the drying process. Certain shades become stronger and deeper—as is the case with dark blue delphinium—while many whites dry the delicate color of parchment. Lily-of-the-valley warms to such an off-white, but dogwood blossoms, feverfew, and daisies usually remain dazzlingly bright. Experiment to discover the color options offered by each new specimen.

SEASONAL CANDIDATES ❧ Though spring, when nature awakens from its winter sleep, is my favorite time of year, it produces very few good candidates for drying. My three favorites are dogwood, lilacs, and peonies. Delicate spring-flowering daffodils, tulips, and pansies tend to reabsorb moisture from the air after a short period of time unless they are encased in an airtight glass dome or frame. Summer and early fall bring the bulk of sun-loving flowers suitable for drying. Some familiar varieties include asters, dahlias, marigolds, roses, sunflowers, zinnias, and button chrysanthemums. In dried flower designs, it's possible to combine flowers from all seasons in one lovely creation (see DELICATE DELIGHT, page 119).

HERBS FOR DESICCANT-DRYING ❧ As an herb fancier, I have found great satisfaction in drying curly green parsley and oregano and chives in bloom. All of these dry in six days when processed with silica gel. The curly green parsley is a special favorite of mine; it provides an unusual background for wreaths and other designs (see CHRISTMAS TREE WREATH, page 183). I usually pot up some parsley plants from my herb garden to keep on my kitchen windowsill all winter. Snipping it now and then makes me feel that a little part of summer is still with me.

HINTS FOR DESICCANT-DRYING

❧ Pastel shades dry best.

❧ Pick roses in the bud to half-open stages.

❧ If a rose has wilted, revive it before drying by recutting the stem end and placing the flower up to its neck in hot water for one hour.

❧ Dahlia-type zinnias dry more attractively than cactus varieties.

❧ 'Envy' zinnias will bloom a deeper green, and dry a more vibrant color, if grown in partial shade.

❧ Peonies should be picked the first day they open.

❧ Pompon dahlias dry better than the cactus-flowered types.

❧ The florets on the top inch of lilac, delphinium, and larkspur spires must be closed for the flower to remain intact when dried.

❧ 'The Fairy' rose and forget-me-nots dry within two days.

❧ All silica-dried blossoms should be wired once cool—see page 200.

DAINTY PASTEL VISION

Tiny things can be beautiful. I fell in love with this dainty candleholder on an antiques hunt and envisioned it on a side table in the farm dining room. In floral design, bigger is often mistaken for better, but when it comes to decorating small spaces, such as apartments or offices, the wide assortment of flower shapes and sizes can be adapted to fit any nook or cranny. Remember that all silica-dried blossoms should be wired once cool.

Materials

Antique candleholder

1 blue six-inch-tall candle

3 pieces florist's foam, 2 -x- 3 inches each

19-gauge florist's wire

Dark green floral tape

2 stems tiny blue delphinium, air-dried

8 short stems pink statice, air-dried

8 short stems white deutzia, leaves attached, silica-dried

12 small pink sweetheart roses, silica-dried

4 white lily-of-the-valley, silica-dried

Instructions

1. Insert candle in antique holder, and stuff small pieces of florist's foam into openings at base of container.
2. Place short sections of delphinium and pink statice in each opening.
3. Using 19-gauge wire and floral tape, wire deutzia stems and insert a few in each opening.
4. Wire roses, and add 6 to front opening, grouping together tightly.
5. Add 3 roses in both of the other side openings.
6. Insert lily-of-the-valley in front opening.

FLOWERED HEART

Filled with a colorful array of summer's flowers, this heart-shaped wreath adds a bit of sun to almost any room. I like the soft touch of the lace bow, but it can be left off, or substituted with a ribbon made from a different fabric, such as faded denim or crushed velvet.

Materials

16-inch-wide, heart-shaped Styrofoam wreath

Sheet moss

36 wire hairpin hooks

19-gauge florist's wire

Dark green floral tape

2 yards three-inch-wide beige lace ribbon

1 wired pick

AIR-DRIED FLOWERS:

16 pink statice

16 white pearly everlasting

2 pink cockscomb

13 pink strawflowers

13 yellow strawflowers

14 white strawflowers

4 blue globe thistle

3 white acroclinium

3 pink acroclinium

SILICA-DRIED FLOWERS:

14 large pink zinnias

6 pink 'Sonia' roses (hybrid teas)

4 blue hydrangeas

22 medium-size maroon zinnias

14 small pink zinnias

Instructions

1. Cover wreath with sheet moss, anchoring moss with wire hairpin hooks (for instructions on how to make hairpin hooks, see page 200).
2. To make a loop for hanging, cut a section of 19-gauge florist's wire, twist ends together, and insert ends into top of Styrofoam.
3. Using the lace ribbon, tie a double-loop bow with streamers; attach to right side of wreath with wired pick.
4. Space large zinnias evenly around face of heart.
5. Place roses and hydrangeas, evenly spaced, about face of heart.
6. Gather statice and pearly everlasting into separate bunches (2 or 3 stems per bunch) and insert around and between roses and large zinnias.
7. Scatter medium-size and small zinnias and cockscomb in empty spaces.
8. Cover any bare spots with strawflowers.
9. Place 4 globe thistle evenly on front of heart (handle carefully to avoid breaking off flower heads).
10. Add acroclinium as accents.

Chapter Five

TRY THE MICROWAVE

Trifles make perfection,

and perfection is no trifle.

MICHELANGELO

WE'VE COME A LONG WAY
since the days when microwave ovens were expensive kitchen luxuries.
And who could have predicted their usefulness for drying flowers? Used
in tandem with silica gel, the microwave can produce remarkable
results, and the speed this method offers is an added bonus.

The flowers best suited for drying in the microwave are those in
the early stages of bloom, free of dew, dampness, and blemishes.
Smaller specimens, such as feverfew, button chrysanthemums, and
miniature marigolds, seem to dry best. Pansies, violets, coralbells,
candytuft, columbine, and other spring flowers dry well in the
microwave, but tend to reabsorb moisture after processing unless they
are enclosed in glass domes or tightly sealed shadow boxes. Lilacs,
coneflowers, viburnum, and dogwood turn dark brown when dried
in the microwave. Dahlias retain a
heavy coating of silica gel desiccant
that can't be removed—even with
an artist's brush—without damaging

*These giant 'Tetra' zinnias produce
branching plants that sometimes
resemble small trees! Due to their
compact, firm blossoms, they are good
candidates for microwave-drying.*

the flower. Delicate flowers that require wired stems, such as daffodils, dry best in the traditional silica gel process because they can't be wired before being dried, and are more likely to shatter if wired after drying in the microwave.

DRYING WITH THE MICROWAVE ❧ Familiarize yourself with your particular microwave before beginning. It is important to note the oven's wattage, size, and number of settings.

Spread a level, one-inch-deep layer of silica gel across the bottom of a glass pie plate or microwave-safe container. Depending on the size of the container and the number of flowers being dried, the amount of desiccant needed will vary, but, in general, a standard-size pie plate requires about one pound of silica gel. It's practical to have on hand a three-pound box of Flower-Dri®.

Arrange flower specimens as you would when drying with desiccant (see Chapter 4, page 58), placing blossoms on one-inch stems face-up or -down, depending on the type of flower, in the silica gel. Space specimens two inches apart and an inch and a half from the sides of the container.

Pour silica gel around the base of the flowers and sprinkle it among the petals carefully to avoid crushing them.

Top with a one-inch covering of silica gel.

Do not cover the dish.

Place one cup of water in a glass in a rear corner of the microwave. Refill the glass as the water is "cooked away." Unless you want to challenge the capabilities of the local fire department, do not overlook this step. Failure to refill the water can lead to a fire.

MICROWAVE DRYING TIME
❧ If your microwave oven has heat settings numbered 1 through 10, use setting 4 (about 300 watts). On a microwave oven with four settings,

MICROWAVE
DRYING TEMPERATURES
in Fahrenheit/Centigrade

ASTILBE	160/70
BACHELOR'S BUTTON	150/65
CANDYTUFT	150/65
COLUMBINE	160/70
CORALBELLS	160/70
COSMOS	150/65
DELPHINIUM	170/75
DEUTZIA*	150/65
HOLLYHOCK	150/65
HYDRANGEA	160/70
MARIGOLD	170/75
MOCK ORANGE*	150/65
ROSE	170/75
SPEEDWELL	170/75
VIOLET	150/65
WINDFLOWER	140/60
YARROW	160/70
ZINNIA	170/75

keep leaves on

place the dial at the midpoint (about 350 watts), and on a microwave with High and Defrost settings, use the Defrost setting (about 200 watts).

There's so much variation in microwave ovens and in the amount of moisture a particular flower contains that it is impossible to predict exact drying times. The number of flowers or leaves being dried together also influences drying time. For instance, two roses contain twice as many water molecules as one, and consequently would require a minute or two longer to dry.

A rough estimate of the drying time for one or more flowers in a half-pound of silica gel is about two-and-a-half minutes. For a more precise calculation, insert a nonmetallic, microwave-safe thermometer into the silica gel, and when it reaches the temperature specified in the chart on page 68, turn off the oven.

To determine the proper setting and microwave-drying time for various flowers, test-dry one flower of each type separately. Based on the number of flowers to be dried together, increase or decrease the standard two-and-a-half-minute drying time accordingly.

REMOVING MICROWAVED FLOWERS

When removing the heated dish containing the processed flowers from the microwave, protect hands with oven mitts or pot holders. Set the container aside to cool for 30 minutes to two hours. Most flowers can be left to cool overnight without any problem. To prevent moisture from forming and becoming reabsorbed, put a lid on the container but leave it open a crack.

If any flowers are still moist, cover them again with silica gel and return the dish to the microwave for a short time on the same setting used initially. It's not necessary to let the desiccant cool prior to reheating, but always allow it to cool between batches of different flowers.

MICROWAVING LEAVES

A variety of leaves are well-suited to microwave-drying. Usually processed for one to two minutes, these desiccant-dried leaves won't be as flexible as they would be if glycerinized (see Chapter 6), but they make nice additions to pictures, small arrangements, and nosegays. See the chart at right for some popular candidates.

LEAVES FOR MICROWAVING

ARTEMISIA 'SILVER QUEEN'

ASTILBE

BEECH

EUCALYPTUS

HOLLYHOCK

HONEY LOCUST

JAPANESE HOLLY

LAMB'S-EARS

LUPINE

MAIDENHAIR FERN

MAPLE

MIMOSA

MULLEIN

OAK

ROSE

GOLDEN TREASURE CHEST

Almost all of the flowers in this design are silica-dried in the microwave. Only the strawflowers and pearly everlasting are hung to dry. Together, they form a compact design of small flowers—the perfect backdrop for a birthday card or *billet-doux*.

Brass or other decorative chest, 7 inches across

1 block florist's foam

19-gauge florist's wire

Dark green floral tape

8 silver-dollar eucalyptus with seedpods, glycerinized

4 yellow sweetheart roses, silica-dried

9 brown-and-yellow, old-fashioned Mexican zinnias, silica-dried

3 gold button zinnias, silica-dried

5 yellow dwarf marigolds—2 single-flowered, 3 double-flowered—silica-dried

5 yellow strawflowers, air-dried

6 bunches white pearly everlasting (2 stems per bunch), air-dried

1. Fill open brass chest with florist's foam, trimmed to fit the container.

2. Outline edge of chest with eucalyptus (for instructions on glycerinization, see Chapter 6): Insert stems directly into foam block.

3. Using 19-gauge wire and floral tape, wire stems for the silica-dried, microwaved flowers (the roses, zinnias, and marigolds).

4. Place roses in center of arrangement as focal points.

5. Surround roses with Mexican zinnias.

6. Fill in empty spaces with strawflowers and button zinnias.

7. Insert single-flowered marigolds near the top of the lid and double-flowered marigolds near the bottom.

8. Wire and tape pearly everlasting bunches and scatter at outer edges of design.

FLOWERING HATBOX

A cheerful combination of yellow hollyhocks and peach roses bursts forth from a floral hat-box. Positioned on a table in a foyer or entrance hall, this warm arrangement invites visitors to take off their own hats and coats, and stay a spell.

Materials

Oval hatbox, 8 inches long
1 block florist's foam
Hot-glue gun and glue sticks
19-gauge florist's wire
Green floral tape

GLYCERINIZED MATERIAL:

6 green-leaf branches of your
    choice

SILICA-DRIED FLOWERS:

2 white peonies
5 peach 'Osiana' roses
3 yellow hollyhocks

AIR-DRIED FLOWERS:

6 white larkspur
9 lavender
3 green amaranthus
2 yellow crested cockscomb
5 brown starflowers
3 green hydrangea
3 dusty rose Joe-Pye weed
6 purple statice
6 yellow craspedia
14 bunches white ammobium
    (3 to 4 stems per bunch)

Instructions

1. Using 19-gauge wire and floral tape, wire stems for the silica-dried, microwaved flowers (the peonies, roses, and hollyhocks).
2. Fill bottom of hatbox with florist's foam, leaving 2 inches extended above rim.
3. Using hot-glue gun, glue cover into florist's foam at an angle on the righthand side.
4. Insert branches of green leaves into florist's foam so that they drape over edges, from right to left (for instructions on glycerinization, see Chapter 6).
5. Form a loose "S" by inserting at a horizontal angle the larkspur, lavender, and amaranthus, so that they sweep upward on the right side and downward on the left side of the arrangement.
6. Fill in lower center area with cockscomb, starting from the bottom upward, and follow with peonies.
7. Add roses as focal points, and accentuate them with starflowers.
8. Fill in any remaining large, open areas with hydrangea and Joe-Pye weed.
9. Place hollyhocks as highlights across top of arrangement.
10. Insert statice at an angle so that it hangs just below rim of hatbox.
11. Scatter craspedia and bunches of ammobium throughout.

Chapter Six

GLYCERINIZATION

I hear the wind among the trees
Playing celestial symphonies,
I see the branches, downward bent,
Like keys of some great instrument.

HENRY WADSWORTH
LONGFELLOW

FOLIAGE PLAYS AN IMPORTANT role in dried flower design, but leafy branches do not respond well to the traditional methods of air- or desiccant-drying. They become brittle and difficult to arrange. But when plants are glycerinized, they remain supple, pliant, even a bit glossy in appearance. Glycerine is an odorless, colorless, syrupy liquid derived from glycerol—a substance used commercially as a solvent or plasticizer. It can be purchased at drugstores in one-pint containers. The glycerinization method of drying is so easy and quick, and the results so enchanting, that all flower lovers should learn how to do it. In fact, the process has become so popular that it is now possible to buy batches of glycerinized eucalyptus branches at supermarkets and florist shops. The object of glycerinization is to keep plants—mostly foliage plants—flexible. A glycerine solution replaces the water content of the plant, allowing it to maintain a natural look and feel when dried.

Decades ago, people used a mixture

When treated with a glycerine solution, peony leaves dry a supple, glossy, dark green. Peony blossoms are best dried in desiccant.

of glycerine and rose water to keep their hands smooth, especially during the harsh winter months. The principle here is the same: Glycerine and water keep leaves soft and help preserve their natural beauty.

PRESERVING LEAFY BRANCHES   As a rule, you should gather six-inch- to two-foot-long branches of deciduous plants and trees in midsummer, when they are mature but still absorbing moisture. Some evergreens, such as boxwood and cedar, can be cut and preserved anytime.

Wash the leaves if they are dirty, and remove any damaged foliage from the branch. Leaves should be free of insect bites or other unsightly blemishes.

Strip any leaves from the lower ends of the branches, and crush the bottom three inches of the woody stems with a hammer to facilitate absorption of the solution.

In a heat-resistant glass jar tall enough to eventually support the branches, mix one part glycerine with two parts very hot water, and stir vigorously to combine. The amount of liquids used varies per container, but, in general, one pint of glycerine plus two pints of water fills three inches of one half-gallon container or two quart-size containers. The solution should be maintained at a three-inch depth. If using a mason jar, large juice bottle, or other screw-top container, close tightly and shake to blend the solution. If using an open-mouth bottle or jar, stir the solution with a spoon. Hot water travels more quickly up the stem than cold, but it is not necessary to boil the water.

Stand the stem ends in the three-inch-deep solution and situate the open jars in a dark, cool place until the leaves change color. Basements are usually too damp, but garages, enclosed porches, or spare rooms are sufficient. The time it takes for leaves to turn varies— from ten days for beech to six to eight weeks for laurel, magnolia, and aspidistra. The resulting color of the leaves varies, too—from brown or soft amber to deep green or dark red—often depending on when the branches were cut and the amount of sunlight they received while growing. For instance, beech branches picked in early July remain greener than those processed in late August. Sunlight fades beech leaves to a pale tan and aspidistra leaves to a pale honey tone. Add vegetable dyes to the glycerine solution to obtain a near match of the original leaf color or to customize colors.

Check the materials periodically to assure that the level of the glycerine solution remains consistent, at a depth of three inches. The solution is absorbed at different rates by different plants, but, in general, it should be replenished every week.

Do not allow the material to stand in the solution for too long or oily beads will appear on the surface of the leaves. If this does occur, remove by wiping off the leaves with damp tissues or washing them under a gentle spray of water. Pat dry.

If leaves appear to wither near their ends when removed from the solution, hang the branches upside down for a few days so the glycerine will run to the tips. Hanging the branches upside down is also the best way to store them.

For added flexibility when arranging, cut off the (approximately three-inch) section of stem that was submerged in the solution and substitute a length of 19-gauge florist's wire, wrapped with dark brown floral tape.

If glycerinized material becomes dusty over time, freshen it up by washing it in tepid water and patting dry.

None of the mixed glycerine solution has to be wasted. Even though it will darken in color, any excess can be used repeatedly, if, when not in use, it is kept in a tightly lidded jar and stored at room temperature. Mildew sometimes forms on the surface, but it does no harm to the solution and can be strained off. When processing plant materials, however, it is essential to replace the absorbed or strained amounts to maintain a three-inch level.

PRESERVING LEAVES AND IVY ❧ Individual leaves, such as those from fatsia and fig, and leafy vines such as ivy are best preserved when completely submerged in the glycerine solution. Lay the specimens in a shallow dish, anchoring them with weights to keep them submerged (a couple of china plates will do the job), and pour in the glycerine-water mixture until the solution is about two- to three-inches deep. The process is relatively rapid, sometimes complete in as little as five to seven days, and so the solution usually does not need to be replenished. After the leaves or vines have darkened, and when they feel flexible and slightly waxy to the touch, remove them from the solution. Wash them with tepid water, pat dry, and spread them out on paper towels to dry thoroughly for several hours. To store, place the vines or leaves between sheets of white tissue paper in a covered box, away from excessive heat.

EXPERIMENTING WITH GLYCERINE ❧ My three favorite plant materials to glycerinize are beech, mountain ash—with its orange berry clusters—and ivy vines. (See BERIBBONED STRAWFLOWER WREATH, using beech branches, page 124; RUSTIC FALL ARRANGEMENT, using mountain ash, page 127; and CUPID LOVES MUSIC, using ivy vines, page 104.) But I do recommend experimenting with new material. You have nothing to lose except a little time and a small quantity of glycerine. Through trial and error, I discovered one summer that blackberry and currant branches preserve well—if they're cut short. The cuttings must be made before the berries are ripe, or they won't remain on the stems. Process as you would leafy branches. After glycerine treatment, spray the berry clusters with hair spray or a clear acrylic sealer.

In my experience, only four varieties of flowers respond quite well to glycerinization. Bells of Ireland is by far the most successful; the blossoms lose their green highlights, but turn a delicate parchment or beige color. The same is true of foxglove and baby's breath. Hydrangeas—picked at full maturity and placed upright in the solution—do fairly well in maintaining some color, although they fare much better when preserved in silica gel.

Tender white buds of Japanese anemone dry a delicate parchment-beige when treated with glycerine. Full blossoms should be processed with a desiccant, as should the neighboring gloriosa daisies and coneflowers.

CANDIDATES FOR GLYCERINIZATION

COMMON NAME	TIME REQUIRED 10-14 DAYS	TIME REQUIRED 4 WEEKS OR MORE	PRESERVED COLOR
ANDROMEDA	✿		Moss-green leaves; beige flower heads
ASPIDISTRA		✿	Brown
BABY'S BREATH	✿		Beige
BEECH	✿		Dark green in July; amber in August
BELLS OF IRELAND	✿		Parchment-beige
BLACKBERRY	✿		Dark green leaves; black berries
BOXWOOD	✿		Forest green
BURNING BUSH	✿		Light green
CHESTNUT	✿		Shades of brown
COTONEASTER	✿		Dark green
CRAB APPLE	✿		Light brown
CURRANT	✿		Dark green leaves; red berries
EUCALYPTUS	✿		Grayish green
FATSIA	✿		Brown
FERNS (pick when spores show)	✿		Dark green
FLAT-LEAF CEDAR		✿	Dark green
FORSYTHIA (without flowers)	✿		Dark green
IVY	✿		Moss-green
JAPANESE ANEMONE	✿		Brown leaves; beige buds
LAUREL	✿		Dark green
LEMON LEAVES	✿		Moss-green
MAGNOLIA		✿	Dark green or mahogany
MAHONIA		✿	Brown
MOUNTAIN ASH	✿		Chocolate-brown; orange berries
NANDINA	✿		Dark brown
OAK	✿		Medium green
PEONY LEAVES (after flowering)	✿		Dark green
VIBURNUM LEAVES	✿		Golden brown

FLOWER-DRYING CHART

COMMON NAME *(Botanical name)*	TIME IN SILICA GEL	TIME TO AIR-DRY	COMMENTS
ACACIA, OR MIMOSA *(Acacia)*	3 days	2 weeks	Leaves air-dry well.
ACROCLINIUM *(Helipterum roseum)*		2 weeks	Pick before flowers are completely open.
AGERATUM *(Ageratum houstonianum)*	3 to 4 days	2 weeks	Flowers dried in silica gel are brighter.
AMARANTHUS *(Amaranthus caudatus)*		3 weeks	Remove leaves for faster drying.
AMMOBIUM, OR WINGED EVERLASTING *(Ammobium alatum)*		2 to 3 weeks	Pick when flowers are no more than half-open.
APPLE (BLOSSOMS AND LEAVES) *(Malus species and hybrids)*	6 to 7 days		Dry leaves and blossoms. Spray twice with a sealer, as blossoms tend to reabsorb moisture.
ARTEMISIA *(Artemisia ludoviciana)*		3 weeks	Pick while tips are still tightly closed and are silvery, or they will turn brownish.
ASTER *(Aster novi-belgii)*	7 days		Dry before flower reaches its peak bloom.
ASTILBE *(Astilbe biternata, or A. davidii)*	3 days	2 weeks	Colors, especially white, stay brighter dried in silica gel.
AZALEA *(Rhododendron)*	6 to 7 days		Wilts gradually unless encased under glass.
BABY'S BREATH *(Gypsophila paniculata)*		2 weeks	Cut when in full flower.
BACHELOR'S BUTTON, OR CORNFLOWER *(Centaurea cyanus)*	5 days	2 to 3 weeks	Pick flowers that have just opened or they will drop their petals after drying.
BELLS OF IRELAND *(Moluccella laevis)*	7 days	3 weeks	Retains brightest green in silica gel. Can also be put in glycerine solution, but becomes parchment-colored.
BITTERSWEET VINE *(Celastrus scandens)*		2 weeks	Pick when orange color is just starting to show in berries. On endangered list in some areas.
BLACK-EYED SUSAN, GLORIOSA DAISY *(Rudbeckia hirta)*	6 to 7 days		Dry large flower heads face-down in silica gel.

COMMON NAME (Botanical name)	TIME IN SILICA GEL	TIME TO AIR-DRY	COMMENTS
BOXWOOD (Buxus)		2 to 3 weeks	Also a great candidate for glycerinization.
BUNNY'S-TAIL GRASS (Lagurus ovatus)		3 weeks	Most effective when stems are bunched together.
BUTTERCUP (Ranunculus acris)	5 days		Also great when pressed.
CALENDULA, OR POT MARIGOLD (Calendula officinalis)	7 days		Reinforce petals by dropping a dab of glue (I recommend Sobo) into center of flower after drying, and spray with hair spray.
CANDYTUFT (Iberis sempervirens)	6 to 7 days		Tends to reabsorb moisture, even after spraying with sealer.
CARNATION (Dianthus caryophyllus)	7 days		Sometimes petals need reinforcing with glue, as for calendula, after being dried.
CATTAIL (Typha angustifolia)		3 weeks	After drying, dip in clear shellac or spray twice with sealer or hair spray.
CHINESE LANTERN (Physalis alkekengi)		3 weeks	Pick before frost and remove leaves before hanging.
CHIVE (FLOWERS) (Allium schoenoprasum)		3 weeks	Pick as soon as flowers open fully.
CHRYSANTHEMUM (Dendranthemum x grandiflorum)	7 days		Button and small daisy mums dry best.
CLARKIA (Clarkia elegans)	7 days	3 weeks	Colors stay brighter in silica gel.
COCKSCOMB, CRESTED (Celosia cristata)		3 weeks	Hang upside down, individually, inside open brown bag for richest colors.
COLUMBINE (Aquilegia canadensis)	7 days		Tends to wilt; spray with hair spray once dried.
CORALBELLS (Heuchera sanguinea)	3 to 4 days		Also great when pressed.
COREOPSIS (Coreopsis tinctoria)	5 to 6 days		Tends to wilt unless put under glass.
COSMOS (Cosmos bipinnatus)	4 to 5 days		Will wilt, even when sprayed, unless sealed under glass.
CRASPEDIA, OR DRUMSTICK (Craspedia globosa)		2 to 3 weeks	Lovely, yellow, drumstick-shaped dried flower.

COMMON NAME *(Botanical name)*	TIME IN SILICA GEL	TIME TO AIR-DRY	COMMENTS
DAFFODIL (LARGE- CUPPED), OR TRUMPET NARCISSUS *(Narcissus pseudonarcissus)*	6 to 7 days		Spray with several coats of sealer or hair spray to prevent wilting.
DAFFODIL (SMALL-CUPPED) *(Narcissus species)*	2 to 3 days		Same as for large-cupped daffodils.
DAHLIA (DWARF) *(Dahlia hybrids)*	7 days		Avoid cactus type. Small pompon varieties are very useful.
DELPHINIUM *(Delphinium elatum)*	7 days	3 weeks	Pick when florets are still closed at least 1 or 2 inches from the tips.
DEUTZIA *(Deutzia)*	5 days		Flowers and leaves dry well, but are dainty and require careful handling.
DOCK *(Rumex crispus)*		2 to 3 weeks	Pick at different stages of color changes: green in June, rosy in July, and brown in August.
DOGWOOD *(Cornus kousa or C. florida)*	5 to 6 days		Dry blossoms separately and glue back onto branches. Apply two coats of hair spray.
DUSTY MILLER *(Senecio cineraria)*	4 to 5 days		Also great when pressed.
EDELWEISS *(Leontopodium alpinum)*	7 days		Pick when flowers are fully open.
FALSE DRAGONHEAD *(Physostegia virginiana)*	7 days		Dry flower head before fully open.
FEVERFEW *(Tanacetum parthenium)*	7 days		Can also be pressed.
FIRETHORN *(Pyracantha coccinea)*	6 to 7 days		Also dries well in glycerine.
FLOWERING QUINCE *(Chaenomeles speciosa)*	6 to 7 days		Spray with hair spray when dry. Holds up better than flowering almond.
FORGET-ME-NOT *(Myosotis sylvatica)*	2 days		Great blue filler for miniature designs.
FORSYTHIA *(Forsythia x intermedia)*	7 days		Pick as soon as flowers open on the branch.
FOXGLOVE *(Digitalis purpurea)*	7 days		When dry, spray with a sealer.

COMMON NAME *(Botanical name)*	TIME IN SILICA GEL	TIME TO AIR-DRY	COMMENTS
FUCHSIA *(Fuchsia hybrids)*	7 days		Stems are weak and need careful wiring.
GAILLARDIA *(Gaillardia amblyodon)*	6 to 7 days		Darkens in color when dry.
GLOBE AMARANTH *(Gomphrena globosa)*		2 weeks	Cut when flowers are completely open.
GLOBE THISTLE *(Echinops exaltatus)*		2 to 3 weeks	Cut when the gray-green heads just begin to turn lavender-blue. Use gloves to handle.
GOLDENROD *(Solidago)*		2 to 3 weeks	Pick early, just as the yellow is starting to show.
HEATHER *(Calluna vulgaris)*		3 weeks	Pick when tips are still closed at least 1 inch from tip of cluster.
HOLLYHOCK *(Alcea rosea)*	7 days		Separate blossoms dry best; spray when dry with 2 coats of hair spray or sealer.
HOP VINE *(Humulus lupulus)*		2 weeks	Pick when fully developed or flowers will shrivel.
HYDRANGEA, BUSH *(Hydrangea macrophylla)*	6 to 7 days	2 weeks	Colors—blue, pink, lavender—dry best in silica gel. Very large heads can be placed face-down, rather than face-up, in silica gel, if necessary.
HYDRANGEA, PEEGEE *(Hydrangea paniculata 'Grandiflora')*		2 weeks	Pick from the pinkish stage onward. Will dry hanging, or upright in an arrangement.
JAPANESE ANEMONE *(Anemone x hybrida)*	4 to 5 days		Buds also dry attractively.
JOE-PYE WEED *(Eupatorium purpureum)*		3 weeks	Pick early, just as the pink is starting to show.
JOHNNY-JUMP-UP *(Viola tricolor)*	2 days		Spray with hair spray. Also great when pressed.
LADY'S MANTLE *(Alchemilla mollis or A. vulgaris)*		2 weeks	Pick while flower heads are still greenish. Leaves are also lovely and can be left on the stems (they will curl a bit).
LAMB'S-EARS *(Stachys byzantina)*		3 weeks	Pick stalks before the flowers mature. Leaves press well.

COMMON NAME (Botanical name)	TIME IN SILICA GEL	TIME TO AIR-DRY	COMMENTS
LARKSPUR (Consolida ambigua)	5 days	3 weeks	Pick when florets are still closed at least 1 inch from the tips.
LAVENDER (Lavandula species and hybrids)		2 to 3 weeks	Cut early, before the buds open to show the tiny flowers.
LIATRIS, OR GAY FEATHER (Liatris spicata)		2 to 3 weeks	Cut when half the flower head has opened.
LILAC (Syringa vulgaris)	7 days		Pick when florets are still closed at least 1 inch from the tips; can be laid horizontally in silica gel.
LILY (Lilium hybrids)	7 days		Just-opened flowers dry best. Handle carefully, as they become fragile when dry.
LILY-OF-THE-VALLEY (Convallaria majalis)	5 days		Turns off-white when dried.
LOVE-IN-A-MIST (Nigella damascena)		2 to 3 weeks	Seedpods dry best and are very useful. Pick 3 to 4 weeks after flowering.
MARIGOLD, DWARF (Tagetes hybrids)	5 days		Pick just at flower's peak.
MARIGOLD, TALL (Tagetes hybrids)	7 days		Pick just at flower's peak. Carefully spoon silica gel between the petals.
MOCK ORANGE (Philadelphus coronarius)	7 days		Spray with hair spray once dry to prevent wilting.
MONEY PLANT, OR HONESTY (Lunaria annua, or L.biennis)		1 to 2 weeks	Can be left to dry on the plant, but pick before seedpods become damaged by wind. Rub pod gently between finger and thumb to reveal shiny disc.
MONKSHOOD (Aconitum napellus)	7 days		New bicolors and deep purples make very effective spikes.
MULLEIN (Verbascum)		3 weeks	Pick when many florets of color are visible.
OAT GRASS (Avena sativa)		3 weeks	For variety, pick in the early green stage and the later golden phase.
OREGANO (FLOWERS) (Origanum vulgare)		3 weeks	Pick early, just-opened, blossoms. Stems harden nicely as they dry.

COMMON NAME (Botanical name)	TIME IN SILICA GEL	TIME TO AIR-DRY	COMMENTS
ORIENTAL POPPY (SEEDPODS) (Papaver orientale)		2 weeks	Flowers are almost impossible to dry, but seedpods are very decorative.
OXEYE DAISY (Leucanthemum vulgare)	4 to 5 days		Place face-down in silica gel. May have to reinforce petals when dry with a drop of craft glue, such as Sobo.
PAMPAS GRASS (Cortaderia selloana)		2 to 3 weeks	Pick as soon as heads are full. Can also be arranged and dried in place.
PANSY (Viola x wittrockiana)	4 days		Tends to wilt in air; give a few coats of hair spray. Also great when pressed.
PARSLEY, CURLY (Petroselinum crispum)	6 days		Dries bright green in silica gel.
PEARLY EVERLASTING (Anaphalis margaritacea)		2 to 3 weeks	Pick early, when in tight bud.
PEONY (Paeonia hybrids)	6 to 7 days	3 weeks	Closed heads and buds can be hung to dry; however, for best results pick the first day flowers open and put in silica gel.
PURPLE CONEFLOWER (Echinacea purpurea)	6 to 7 days		Dries a deeper shade, but very lovely.
PUSSY WILLOW (Salix discolor)		2 weeks	Pick when some silver catkins are closed on ends. Can be dried upright in an arrangement or hung upside down.
QUEEN ANNE'S LACE (Daucus carota)	5 days	2 weeks	Can be hung to dry, but stays whiter and more open in silica gel.
RANUNCULUS (Ranunculus asiaticus)	7 days		Must be given 2 coats of sealer to prevent wilting.
ROSE, MINIATURE (Rosa hybrids)	3 to 4 days		Pick when flowers are no more than half-open.
ROSE, TEA-TYPE (Rosa species and hybrids)	6 to 7 days		Pick when flowers are no more than half-open. Avoid dark red roses, which dry black.
ROSE, 'THE FAIRY' (Polyantha rose)	2 days		Pick before flower cluster is fully open.
SALVIA, BLUE (Salvia farinacea)		2 to 3 weeks	Tie in small bunches before hanging to dry.

COMMON NAME (Botanical name)	TIME IN SILICA GEL	TIME TO AIR-DRY	COMMENTS
SEA LAVENDER, OR CASPIA (Limonium latifolium)		3 weeks	Pick when flower head has just opened.
SEDUM 'AUTUMN JOY' (Hylotelephium telephium x H. spectabile)		3 weeks	Pick when flower heads have developed enough to become firm. Hang in small bunches, as stems take a long time to dry.
SHASTA DAISY (Leucanthemum x superbum)	7 days		Very useful, white, dried flower.
SILVER-DOLLAR EUCALYPTUS (Eucalyptus polyanthemos)		3 weeks	For flexibility, process with glycerine.
SILVER LACE VINE (Polygonum aubertii)	6 days		Pick just as the billowing flowers begin to open.
SNAPDRAGON (Antirrhinum majus)	7 to 8 days		Good spiky addition to arrangements.
SPIDER FLOWER (Cleome hasslerana)	6 days		Very delicate: Dry individually, upright in large coffee cans, for best results.
STARFLOWER (Scabiosa stellata)		2 to 3 weeks	Pick when flower heads are light brown balls.
STATICE, ANNUAL (Limonium sinuatum)		3 weeks	Pick the first day the flower heads open.
STATICE, GERMAN, OR PERENNIAL (Goniolimon tataricum or Limonium tataricum)		1 week	Perennial statice dries very rapidly.
STATICE, RUSSIAN, OR RATTAIL (Psylliostachys suworowii or Limonium suworowii)		3 weeks	Pick when pink color appears and before all the blossoms are fully open. Dries mauve in color.
STRAWFLOWER (Helichrysum bracteatum)		2 weeks	Place buds on wires; as they dry, they open and anchor to the wire.
SUNFLOWER (Helianthus annuus)	7 to 9 days		Pick blossoms as soon as they open. It may be necessary to further dry the center in the air after removal from silica gel.
SWEET ALYSSUM (Lobularia maritima)	2 to 3 days		Great for pressed-flower pictures, including the stems.

COMMON NAME *(Botanical name)*	TIME IN SILICA GEL	TIME TO AIR-DRY	COMMENTS
SWEET WILLIAM *(Dianthus barbatus)*	7 days		Pick newly opened flower heads to dry.
TANSY *(Tanacetum vulgare)*		3 weeks	Pick before heads start to darken to brown. Retains a pungent odor.
TRUMPET VINE *(Campsis radicans)*	7 to 9 days		Wire and spray flower heads with hair spray.
TULIP *(Tulipa hybrids)*	7 days		Dry each tulip upright in a paper cup to best retain the shape. When removed, spray twice with hair spray.
VERBENA *(Verbena x hortensis)*	6 days		Dark colors tend to fade. Each floret presses nicely.
VERONICA, OR SPEEDWELL *(Veronica species and hybrids)*	5 days	2 weeks	Retains color best in silica gel.
VIBURNUM *(Viburnum prunifolium)*	7 days		Leaves preserve well in glycerine.
VIOLET *(Viola odorata)*	4 to 5 days		Very delicate when dry and tends to reabsorb moisture.
WEIGELA *(Weigela florida)*	5 to 6 days		Flowers tend to wilt. Spray with sealer immediately after removing from silica gel.
WHEAT *(Triticum aestivum)*		3 weeks	Harvest promptly to avoid wind/rain damage.
WINDFLOWER *(Anemone species)*	4 to 5 days		Spray twice with sealer, as they tend to reabsorb moisture.
XERANTHEMUM *(Xeranthemum annuum)*		2 to 3 weeks	Pick flowers at all stages to dry—buds, half-open, or fully open.
YARROW, GOLDEN *(Achillea millefolium hybrids)*		3 weeks	Spray heavily with hair spray or sealer.
YARROW, PASTELS *(Achillea millefolium hybrids)*	6 to 7 days		Colors dry best in silica gel, but can be hung to dry if being used as a filler flower.
ZINNIA, GIANT *(Zinnia elegans hybrids)*	6 to 7 days		Pastel shades dry best.
ZINNIA, SMALL *(Zinnia elegans hybrids)*	4 to 5 days		Avoid dark tones, except for lovely Mexican types.

part three
THE DESIGN

Chapter Seven
THE VICTORIAN STYLE

Here is a brighter garden,
Where not a frost has been,
In its unfading flowers
I hear the bright bee hum;
Prithee, my brother,
Into my garden come!

EMILY DICKINSON

VICTORIA WAS CROWNED QUEEN of England in 1837 and ruled until 1901, but her influence persists well into the twentieth century. It can still be seen in ornate, floral-patterned curtains, wall papers, carpets, and furnishings. During the Victorian era, an obsession with flowers extended into every arena of life. Elaborate fresh and dried arrangements decorated the home, specific planting plans dictated the layout of the garden, and an entire language of flowers determined which blossoms were placed together in a bouquet to express certain sentiments. In more ways than one, flowers made a statement.

Serious gardening was considered too dirty a business for proper Victorian ladies, but the well-educated woman was expected to be knowledgeable on the subject of flowers. By the end of the nineteenth century, finishing schools offered instruction in botany, "florigraphy" (the language of flowers), and the assemblage of nosegays. Flowers were cut daily for

This elaborate arrangement typifies the Victorian style: Richly colored cockscombs, delphiniums, hydrangeas, and larkspur burst forth from an ornately carved container.

display indoors. The arrangements tended to be rather ostentatious, accompanied by numerous accessories and knickknacks, but they exuded a certain warmth and charm, cluttered as they were. Many Victorian flower designs were placed under glass domes to protect them from the ever-present coal and fireplace dust. Some of these domed designs can be found today in antiques stores, still intact, if lacking vivid color.

In Victorian times, flowers were dried for winter use and for fashioning "tussie-mussies," or nosegays. The nosegay is probably the most enduring legacy of nineteenth-century flower-arranging. Every "respectable" Victorian woman had several posy holders—cone-shaped funnels made of silver or filigree. The "tussie" was a cluster of flowers, usually with at least one rose in the center, kept fresh by a "mussie"—a moistened piece of moss. Each flower symbolized certain sentiments, and the complete arrangement was endlessly analyzed by its recipient in an attempt to decipher its meaning. The petite bouquets were carried in the ornate posy holders or wrapped in fine lace, doilies, or leaves tied with ribbons. The smallest ones could be attached to the bodice of a gown.

Victorians delighted in presenting flowers that expressed special messages of passion, friendship, or sympathy. In addition to the mania for tussie-mussie making, they enjoyed fashioning pictures, calling cards, and bookmarks from pressed flowers.

Containers resembling cupids and cherubs, compact baskets, and formal vases were popular, as were hatboxes. Dried herbs and homegrown fruit were often incorporated into floral designs, as were peacock feathers, for which Victorians had a tremendous fascination. Rich colors were used, and the elegant designs were often wider than they were tall.

COLORS OF THE VICTORIAN AGE ❦ Victorian colors were deep, rich, and bold: magenta, mustard, purple, royal blue, and dark crimson. Furniture and woodwork were rendered in somber tones of mahogany and rosewood. To counterbalance the somewhat solemn atmosphere of the rooms, large flower arrangements usually incorporated bright colors rather than pastels. Wicker and wooden plant stands helped to further brighten dimly lit parlors and drawing rooms.

FLOWERS FOR A VICTORIAN LOOK ❦ Many of the flowers favored by Victorians are readily available. The rose, particularly the cabbage rose, was evident everywhere—indoors, carved or printed on furnishings, and outdoors, in the garden. Sunflowers, so popular today, were then considered a symbol of constancy, and appeared on andirons and on mantel and building facades. Legend has it that Oscar Wilde regularly wore a sunflower as a *boutonnière*. Other popular flowers from the period include annuals such as cockscomb, globe amaranth, larkspur, and verbena, and perennials such as delphinium, hollyhock, lavender, peony, and bush hydrangea. These flowers all retain their colors when dried and can be fashioned into wreaths, garlands, nosegays, and bouquets.

ESSENTIALS OF VICTORIAN ARRANGEMENTS ❦ Arrangements designed in the Victorian style are generally opulent and massed with vibrant, colorful flowers. For the outline, assemble long, spiky flowers such as 'Silver King' artemisia, delphinium, larkspur, and bells of Ireland. For full-blossomed focal flowers, use crested cockscomb,

peonies, and roses. Baby's breath, feverfew, and strawflower make excellent fillers. Depending upon the choice of container, decide on a place to position the finished arrangement. I personally prefer to create Victorian-style arrangements in decorative bowl and pitcher sets (see VIOLET BOWL AND PITCHER, page 109). Elaborate candleholders and lamp bases are also suitable. After filling the container with dry florist's foam that extends two inches above the rim, insert spiky materials first, to provide the overall dimensions of the design. Next add the large accent flowers. Finish by filling in any open spaces with smaller, airy blooms and bits of foliage.

A bashful boy and girl peek out over a small pond surrounded by blooming foxglove, delphinium, loosestrife, and lilies. Victorian figurines make enchanting focal points in flowering gardens.

THE LANGUAGE OF FLOWERS

ARTEMISIA 'SILVER KING' . . . . power, dignity	IVY . . . . friendship, matrimony
BABY'S BREATH . . . . pure heart	LARKSPUR . . . . ardent attachment
BELLS OF IRELAND . . . . whimsy	LAVENDER . . . . luck, success
BUTTERCUP . . . . cheerfulness, childishness	PANSY . . . . thoughts
CHRYSANTHEMUM . . . . optimism	PEONY . . . . bashfulness
COCKSCOMB . . . . silliness, humor	ROSE . . . . love
DAHLIA . . . . gratitude	ROSEMARY . . . . remembrance
DAISY . . . . innocence	SUNFLOWER . . . . . . loyalty, adoration
DELPHINIUM . . . . well-being	WHEAT . . . . abundance
FEVERFEW . . . . good health	VERBENA . . . . fidelity
GLOBE AMARANTH . . . . . . immortality	VIOLET . . . . modesty
HOLLYHOCK . . . . fruitfulness	YARROW . . . . soothes sorrows
HYDRANGEA . . . . devotion	ZINNIA . . . . thoughts of absent friends

LACE FAN AND LAVENDER BUNCH

Hung on a wall, propped on a bedroom pillow, set on a night table—this versatile lace fan will suggest warm sentiments wherever it's placed. Little lavender flowers seem so unassuming, but, when bunched together, they emit an enduring aroma that's sure to melt even the coldest of hearts. What better accessories for little ones playing dress-up on a rainy afternoon!

Materials

Lace fan form with Oasis holder (available at craft shops)

1 yard one-inch-wide lace ribbon

1½ yards pink-and-white ribbon

½ yard one-inch-wide pink wired-ribbon

1 wired pick

19-gauge florist's wire

Green floral tape

Rubber band

6 lemon leaves, glycerinized

30 lavender stems, fresh

AIR-DRIED FLOWERS:

7 pink larkspur

7 blue larkspur

3 small maroon crested cockscomb

4 white strawflowers

3 pink strawflowers

5 purple statice

5 white ammobium clusters, (2 to 3 stems per bunch)

SILICA-DRIED FLOWERS:

1 pink hollyhock with bud

3 'Bridal Pink' roses, with buds

6 pink 'Peter Pan' zinnias

Instructions

1. Insert lemon leaves into Oasis holder to create background for flowers.
2. Place larkspur in front of lemon leaves, alternating colors.
3. Tie one bow from lace and pink-and-white ribbons by holding both together. Wire to pick and insert at bottom of fan.
4. Just above the bow, insert the largest of the 3 cockscomb. Insert 2 smaller ones several inches above.
5. Using 19-gauge wire and floral tape, wire stems for the silica-dried flowers.
6. Near the center of the arrangement, add roses, with a few buds toward the top.
7. Insert zinnias around roses, working from the bottom upward.
8. Place strawflowers toward the outer edges of the design.
9. Use statice and ammobium to fill in sparse spots.
10. To make lavender bunch: Tie fresh stems together with rubber band; wrap with pink wired-ribbon, covering band; make bow; push hollyhock under bow. Bunch air-dries as is.

VICTORIAN WREATH

Celebrate the success of your cutting garden by creating a wreath out of the wide variety of blossoms you've grown and dried. This Victorian-style wreath is a showstopper, vibrant with reds and greens; flowers are placed so close together they cover every inch of the form. The recipe for the accompanying arrangement is on the following page.

Materials

24-inch-diameter Styrofoam wreath form

Green sheet moss

Hairpin hooks

Spool-wire

19-gauge florist's wire

Green floral tape

2 yards three-inch-wide gold wired-ribbon

1 crystal or other decorative ornament

2 wired picks

AIR-DRIED FLOWERS:

8 green hydrangea

5 maroon cockscomb

29 gold yarrow

3 white strawflowers

3 pink strawflowers

3 maroon strawflowers

45 white pearly everlasting

1 bunch white German statice

SILICA-DRIED FLOWERS:

3 pale pink peonies

3 maroon peonies

48 zinnias, large- and small-flowered, in shades ranging from pink to maroon

12 pink roses

3 purple asters

Instructions

1. Cover wreath form with sheet moss using hairpin hooks (for instructions on how to make hooks, see page 200).

2. To make a loop for hanging, cut a section of 19-gauge florist's wire, twist ends together, and insert ends into top of Styrofoam.

3. Tie a large double bow with the gold wired-ribbon and attach it to top of wreath with a wired pick. Gather streamers on each side with spool-wire.

4. Space hydrangea evenly throughout wreath.

5. Using 19-gauge wire and floral tape, wire stems for the silica-dried flowers.

6. Position peonies, large-flowered zinnias, and cockscomb around the wreath, loosely alternating placement for a variety of color throughout.

7. Tuck in roses and yarrow.

8. Use small-flowered zinnias, strawflowers, asters, pearly everlasting, and German statice as fillers to give the wreath an abundant, full look.

9. Secure decorative ornament to center of wreath with remaining wired pick.

VICTORIAN VASE

An ornate, very Victorian-style vase complements the lush colors of the dried blooms it contains. Bright green hydrangeas and warm pink peonies mirror the colors in the Victorian wreath featured on the preceding page, making for a distinctive duo.

Materials

Victorian-style or other decorative vase

1 block florist's foam

19-gauge florist's wire

Green floral tape

Decorative ornament

AIR-DRIED FLOWERS:

14 'Silver King' artemisia

5 green hydrangea

3 pink crested cockscomb

SILICA-DRIED FLOWERS:

7 bells of Ireland

5 white Japanese peonies, with several buds

5 pink Japanese peonies, with several buds

9 'Heart's Delight' roses, or other bicolor roses

6 'Envy' zinnias

Instructions

1. Pack florist's foam into vase, leaving 2 inches extended above rim.
2. Using 19-gauge wire and floral tape, wire stems for the silica-dried flowers.
3. Form the outline of the design with bells of Ireland and artemisia.
4. Insert hydrangea and cockscomb.
5. Add 9 peonies, reserving 1 pink blossom.
6. Scatter roses and zinnias throughout arrangement.
7. Accessorize vase by placing the remaining pink peony at its base, accompanied by a decorative ceramic, glass, or crystal ornament such as the grapes shown in the photograph.

CHERUB SWAG

A playful cherub, surrounded by ferns, peonies, and lilacs, peeks down from his perch. This exquisite yet easy-to-make swag looks as lovely on top of a bookcase or mantel as it does here on a china cabinet. The color scheme can be modified by substituting blue hydrangeas and maroon peonies.

Materials

1 block Styrofoam or florist's foam

Floral adhesive (such as Fantastik, available at craft shops)

19-gauge florist's wire

Dark olive-green floral tape

1 cherub statue

GLYCERINIZED MATERIAL:

4 birch branches

5 Ming fern branches

SILICA-DRIED FLOWERS:

2 white hydrangea

7 pink peonies and 1 bud stem

9 lilacs

AIR-DRIED FLOWERS:

5 green hop vines

3 bunches white pearly everlasting (30 individual stems)

Instructions

1. Using floral adhesive, attach foam block to the top right, front edge of cabinet or shelf.
2. To create a sturdy, sweeping motion for the swag, insert 2 birch branches on each side of the foam block, with those on the right side cascading out over the cabinet corner and downward.
3. Using 19-gauge wire and floral tape, wire stems for the silica-dried flowers.
4. Set cherub on top of foam block, and flank with hydrangea.
5. Add Ming fern and hop vines.
6. Add peonies and lilacs throughout arrangement (refer to photograph on following page for placement).
7. Tuck in bunches of pearly everlasting to complete the flowing design.

CUPID LOVES MUSIC

Inspire romantic feelings with this sweeping portrait in pastels. Just a touch of dark lavender in the anemones and grapes provides dramatic contrast to the soft strands of silver lace vine and the delicate pink bells of the foxglove. The white of the daisies clarifies the other colors in the design.

Materials

Cupid urn

1 block florist's foam

Sheet moss

Hairpin hooks or wire fasteners

19-gauge florist's wire

Green floral tape

Spool-wire

2 long picks

2 bunches decorative purple grapes

GLYCERINIZED MATERIAL:

13 maidenhair fern fronds

7 ivy strands

SILICA-DRIED FLOWERS:

8 trailing dusty miller stems

5 silver lace vine strands

3 pink foxglove

11 pink-and-lavender dahlias

5 Shasta daisies

5 purple anemones

AIR-DRIED FLOWERS:

10 light purple statice

20 bicolor globe amaranth

18 white pearly everlasting

Instructions

1. Cut block of florist's foam to fill urn. Cover with sheet moss and secure with hairpin hooks or wire fasteners (for instructions on how to make hooks, see page 200).
2. Using 19-gauge wire and floral tape, wire stems for the silica-dried flowers.
3. Create the line of the arrangement by inserting fern fronds, ivy strands, dusty miller stems, silver lace vine, and foxgloves in descending order, with highest point to the far left and lowest to the far right.
4. Using picks, insert bunches of grapes—one hung below the rim of the container and slightly to the right of center; the other above the rim and left of center.
5. Place largest dahlia in front center at base of arrangement. Set remaining dahlias above and to the right and left of the focal dahlia.
6. Scatter daisies throughout, to echo the white of the container.
7. Insert anemones in a triangular pattern.
8. Add statice in between the dahlias.
9. Fill in bare spots with globe amaranth and pearly everlasting, wired together with spool-wire and inserted in bunches.

VICTORIAN COCOA POT

The color, shape, and size of a container can serve as guidelines when determining which flowers to include in an arrangement. Decorative tin cans or rough-hewn wooden bins may suggest a free-form of wildflowers. The yellow and pink rose pattern on this antique cocoa pot is repeated in its more formal arrangement.

Materials

Cocoa pot
1 block florist's foam
19-gauge florist's wire
Green floral tape

GLYCERINIZED MATERIAL:
7 silver-dollar eucalyptus
    branches

SILICA-DRIED FLOWERS:
2 yellow snapdragons
3 'Golden Masterpiece' roses
4 pink 'Queen Elizabeth' roses

AIR-DRIED FLOWERS:
9 pink larkspur
10 'Silver King' artemisia
5 pink Russian statice
5 green amaranthus
2 maroon crested cockscomb
5 green hydrangea
9 purple statice
3 gold yarrow
14 pink globe amaranth

Instructions

1. Firmly position florist's foam in cocoa pot, leaving 2 inches extended above rim.
2. Using 19-gauge wire and floral tape, wire stems for the silica-dried flowers.
3. Use larkspur, artemisia, Russian statice, amaranthus, and snapdragons to form the outline of the design.
4. Add cockscomb and hydrangea to the center of the arrangement (refer to photograph for placement).
5. Arrange roses around cockscomb.
6. Fill in empty spaces with purple statice, yarrow, and small bunches of globe amaranth (2 or 3 stems per bunch).
7. Insert eucalyptus branches last, fanning out from the back of the design.

VIOLET BOWL AND PITCHER

A scattering of cheerful Shasta daisies, 'Blue Moon' and 'Heart's Delight' roses, and clusters of silk violets create a stunning combination when arranged in a pretty, floral-patterned pitcher set. (Violets are not good candidates for drying, but silk violets make an excellent substitute for the real thing.)

Materials

Bowl and pitcher set, decorated with violets

1 block florist's foam

19-gauge florist's wire

Green floral tape

5 silk violet clusters, wired (available at craft stores)

12 pepper berry stems, wired (available at floral supply outlets)

AIR-DRIED FLOWERS:

6 purple delphinium

10 silvery caspia

9 white larkspur

8 rose heather

6 pink Russian statice

2 maroon crested cockscomb

3 purple hydrangea

36 white strawflowers, air-dried

SILICA-DRIED FLOWERS:

8 'Blue Moon' (purple) roses

3 'Heart's Delight' (bicolor) roses

12 Shasta daisies

GLYCERINIZED MATERIAL:

7 maidenhair fern fronds

Instructions

1. Fill pitcher with florist's foam, leaving 2 inches extended above rim.
2. Using 19-gauge wire and floral tape, wire stems for the silica-dried flowers.
3. Form the outline of the arrangement with delphinium, caspia, larkspur, heather, and Russian statice.
4. Insert cockscomb and hydrangeas, working from the bottom of the design upward.
5. Place purple and bicolor roses as focal points, near the base and center.
6. Scatter Shasta daisies throughout.
7. Add accents of pepper berry stems.
8. Make bunches of strawflowers by wrapping the wires of 6 or 7 together with floral tape, so that each bunch will conform in size with the rest of the flowers in the arrangement. Insert the bunches in between the dark colored focal flowers.
9. Add the silk violets in a triangular pattern, to reflect the design on the pitcher.
10. Place airy maidenhair fern fronds around the back and sides.

FOR HAND & MACHINE
SPOO COTTON

Chapter Eight

ARRANGEMENTS FOR ALL SEASONS

*Every artist dips his brush
in his own soul, and paints his
own nature into his pictures.*

HENRY WARD BEECHER

ALL FOUR SEASONS HAVE MEANING in the life of a garden. The sun coaxes each new bud to speak the secret of spring. Summer spreads the word with glorious outbursts of blossoms. Fall reaps the rewards of nature's labors. And winter offers a chance for silence, for sleep.

Flowers and plants can be combined to create designs that showcase the distinctive features of each season. A little forethought will allow for enough materials to create stunning dried arrangements year-round. In spring, flowering shrubs such as forsythia and lilac extend graceful branches for eye-catching designs. Summer, with its abundance of roses, sunflowers, and zinnias, presents a veritable rainbow of colors. The full, ripe vegetables of fall make for hearty arrangements when combined with berried vines and burnished leaves. Fragrant pine cones, crisp holly leaves, and sprightly ivy branches bring a touch of green to any winter scene.

This flowering acacia "tree" states quite simply that spring has arrived. Delicate yellow blossoms and silver-dollar eucalyptus leaves are fixed atop a "trunk" fashioned from grapevine bark, while tulips decorate the base.

SPRING

Spring is a time of renewal for gardeners and flower lovers. Winter's once-barren landscapes begin to show signs of growth. Buds burst forth from branches and birds twitter from treetops, encouraging gardeners to get down to the business of planting. The colors associated with this uplifting season are predominantly yellows, whites, and greens.

SPRING FLOWERS FOR DRYING ⊱ Only a few spring flowers can be air-dried: heather, lavender, mimosa, and pussy willow. Most spring flowers—especially spring-flowering bulbs—have waxy, succulent petals that do not lend themselves to air-drying. Azaleas, daffodils, narcissus, pansies, ranunculus, tulips, and vibernum are best preserved in silica gel. Because they have a tendency to reabsorb moisture after a few weeks, they will last longer if their arrangements are encased under glass or in shadow boxes. Several coats of hair spray or clear acrylic also help prolong their beauty.

Lilacs and peonies are two old-fashioned, reliable, spring favorites that are well-suited to preserving in silica gel. Hybrid lilacs come in many shades, but I still prefer the traditional purple blossoms. Cut the stems when the buds at least one inch from the tips of the flower clusters are still tightly closed. This way, the fragrance will be preserved along with the flower. Peonies—all forms, from the old-fashioned, fragrant, double-flowered varieties to the Japanese single and crested types—should be picked the first day they open fully. Deep red cultivars retain their color exceptionally well in silica gel and add much impact to a design, especially since most spring colors tend to be pale.

BRANCHES IN BLOOM ⊱ The lavish display of spring-blooming shrubs and trees is fleeting, so blossoms should be dried whenever possible to extend their delicate beauty. Forced branches of shrubs and trees, such as forsythia, flowering cherry, and dogwood, serve to fill the dreary period between winter and spring. Place the cut, crushed stems in tepid water, gradually increasing the amount of light exposure, and in less than two weeks, the buds will burst forth. Short flower clusters of forsythia dry in silica gel after one week. Once dried, attach them to bare branches with a hot-glue gun or floral tape. Individual cherry and dogwood flowers dry in silica gel in six to seven days. For a natural effect, glue blossoms back onto branches, and arrange with other spring flowers, including bells of Ireland, in a visual symphony of spring (see ST. PATRICK'S DAY BOWL, page 164).

The color green is essential to any spring arrangement. In the arrangement featured on page 110, stems of green silver-dollar eucalyptus add just the right touch to a "mimosa tree." The tree is fashioned

Mother Nature is at her most prolific in summer: Pink phlox and foxglove, red hollyhock, and yellow coreopsis frame terraced farmland.

from grapevine bark. Flowering branches of mimosa—some hung to dry, others processed in silica gel—are inserted into a ball of dry florist's foam to form its canopy. White-flowering branches of the deutzia bush, dried in silica gel, would make another effective spring "tree."

SUMMER

Summer is nature's most prolific season. A multitude of flowers in bright, bold colors can be used to create lavish displays. Bring some of these sun-drenched shades indoors to enjoy in fresh designs and to preserve for splendid dried creations. Pick the most perfect specimens for drying, and do so without remorse—visualizing the setting in which they will be enjoyed all winter long makes snipping that much easier.

SUMMER FLOWERS FOR DRYING Unlike spring, summer brings many flowers that can simply be air-dried: ageratum, amaranthus, artemisia, baby's breath, bachelor's button, cockscomb, delphinium, globe amaranth, larkspur, statice, strawflower, and yarrow. With a little help from silica gel, dahlias, marigolds, roses, Shasta daisies, snapdragons, sunflowers, and zinnias can all be added to the list of summer's offerings.

The dried-flower designer has the option of mixing flowers and herbs from different seasons into one design, as shown in the CHRISTMAS CAROUSEL HORSE on page 192. Such a combination effectively bridges the gap that nature set between them.

FALL

As autumn approaches, berries grace stems of bittersweet, nandina, and pyracantha. Chinese lanterns bloom along with many-shaded chrysanthemums. Fall is frequently a melancholic time: The still of winter is not far behind, and summer burns out in a blaze of glory. The woods are alive with fiery colors, each leaf a lit match, extinguished in slow motion. Autumn's striking contrasts are showcased in the RUSTIC FALL ARRANGEMENT on page 127, where berried vines, turning leaves, fruits, and vegetables are accented with Chinese lanterns.

FALL PLANTS FOR DRYING Supple branches and vines can be fashioned into wreaths by simply circling them around wire frames and wrapping the stems in place with spool-wire. Lay the wreaths flat to dry for several weeks, then hang to enjoy.

Peegee hydrangea flower heads lend themselves to wreath-making and will dry in place.

The drying process does produce some shrinkage, however, so use an excess of materials. If necessary, smaller pieces can be added to fill in any holes after the drying process is complete.

Gather some wild grasses, oats, wheat, corn, and seed heads to use in "cornucopious" fall designs. These wildings blend in beautifully with the warm colors that epitomize the season.

The onset of autumn signals that Jack Frost will soon close the garden gate and scatter his icy coating over all of Mother Nature's flowers. Frost strikes at different times in different parts of the country, but, at my farm in upstate New York, it usually arrives by mid-September. Not all of the planted areas are blackened with this first frost: More than once over the years I've continued to harvest dahlias and snapdragons well into October.

Fall is also the time to pot up any preferred herb plants and bring them indoors to grow on kitchen windowsills. My personal favorites, curly parsley and basil, are always good choices. Since I use lots of curly parsley in my dried arrangements and wreaths, I pick it regularly for preserving in silica gel.

WINTER

Winter calls for resourcefulness. Gardens are dormant, but the preserved bounty from seasons past serves to brighten the interior of a home or office now void of fresh-cut blossoms. The approaching holiday season encourages creativity with combinations of fresh and treated evergreens, pine cones, fruits, nuts, foliage, and candles. And I love picking rose hips and branches of scarlet winterberry and holly to use in traditional arrangements. Never hesitate to experiment with combinations of fresh, dried, silk, and treated materials.

After the killing frost, I usually gather all the dead plants and clean the flower beds. Roses are "hilled" (their crowns covered with soil), peonies, delphiniums, and other perennials are cut back, and dahlias and gladiolus bulbs are dug up and stored in peat moss. A coating of well-rotted cow manure or organic material acts as a top-dressing. It will further decompose over the winter months and be dug under in early spring.

A SEASON OF PLANNING ❧ Just when the winter doldrums set in after the hectic holidays, seed catalogs start arriving daily in the mail. Study them carefully to see what new avenues seem appealing for next year's garden. Order different varieties of flowers—not just for drying purposes, but also to expand the garden plan. Sketch a plan of action, perhaps one that includes a small section in which your children or grandchildren can plant a few flowers. Gardening can be a great family activity. Put your dreams on paper during the stark winter months and watch them materialize into a panorama of color come spring.

SPRING FANTASY

When used as containers, ordinary garden tools such as bushel baskets, milking pails, even wheelbarrows, can bring a touch of country to any interior. Here, an old-fashioned, copper-bottomed watering can displays all the signs of spring for months of enjoyment indoors—long after the daffodils, tulips, and lilacs have disappeared for another year.

Materials

Watering can
1 block florist's foam
19-gauge florist's wire
Dark green floral tape

AIR-DRIED FLOWERS:
5 'Silver Mound' artemisia, with short stems
14 acacia branches
7 pussy willow branches

SILICA-DRIED FLOWERS:
6 yellow forsythia branches
6 white tulips
6 yellow tulips
12 yellow daffodils
5 lilacs

Instructions

1. Secure florist's foam in watering can, leaving 2 inches extended above rim.
2. Using 19-gauge wire and floral tape, wire stems for the silica-dried flowers.
3. Cover florist's foam with artemisia, sticking stems directly into foam.
4. Insert forsythia and acacia branches so that they form a sweeping curve of open, airy dimensions.
5. Place tulips and daffodils throughout the center of the arrangement, from bottom to top.
6. Set lilacs into outer edges of arrangement.
7. Insert pussy willow branches as accents.

DELICATE DELIGHT

Delphiniums, larkspur, zinnias, and roses—the flowers of spring and summer are featured in this eye-catching creation. A sprightly green bow pulls the look together. Place this arrangement on a guest-room dresser, dining-room sideboard, or rec-room windowsill.

Materials

Large vase with decorative handle

1 block florist's foam

2 yards three-inch-wide green wired-ribbon

long wired pick

19-gauge florist's wire

Dark green floral tape

9 lemon leaves, glycerinized

AIR-DRIED FLOWERS:

12 'Silver King' artemisia

12 delphinium, ranging in color from light to dark blue

16 pink larkspur

7 pink 'Floradale' crested cockscomb

5 gold yarrow

3 rosy pink Peegee hydrangea

SILICA-DRIED FLOWERS:

3 pale blue hydrangea

1 pink hydrangea

6 pink peonies

3 white peonies

4 pale pink 'Tetra' zinnias

8 'Bridal Pink' roses

Instructions

1. Fill vase with florist's foam, leaving 2 inches extended above rim.
2. Using 19-gauge wire and floral tape, wire stems for the silica-dried flowers.
3. Tie a double bow with the ribbon and wire it onto pick. Insert near handle.
4. Insert artemisia, delphinium, and larkspur towards back of arrangement, to create height.
5. Position cockscomb, on their own stems, with the largest at base of arrangement, the others about 4 to 5 inches above base.
6. Add hydrangea to the right and left of center.
7. Space peonies, zinnias, and roses so that larger flowers are closer to base and smaller blooms are nearer to outside edges and top of arrangement.
8. Fill bare spaces with yarrow and Peegee hydrangea.
9. Using 19-gauge wire and floral tape, wire lemon leaves and place around outer back side to frame design.

RUGGED ROCKS AND BRANCHES

Rough, earthy materials such as rocks, mushrooms, and cotton-boll branches are combined to create a southwestern—even masculine—look. The result is well-suited to a rec room or family library. It also makes an interesting centerpiece for a country kitchen table.

Materials

4 flat rocks

1 three-inch-diameter needlepoint holder (available at craft and floral supply stores)

Sheet moss

2 wood picks

1 protea (available at floral supply stores)

1 large sunflower, silica-dried

1 small sunflower, silica-dried

2 woodland fungus, or mushrooms, air-dried

4 poppy seedpods, air-dried

6 popcorn tree (also known as Tyler tree) branches, air-dried

5 branches of cotton bolls, air-dried

Instructions

1. Select a spot to display the finished arrangement, and place flat rocks around needlepoint holder. (For a portable arrangement, set upon large tray.)
2. Cover areas between rocks with sheet moss.
3. Using 19-gauge wire and floral tape, wire stems for the silica-dried flowers.
4. Skewer mushrooms with picks and insert in needlepoint holder on right rear side.
5. Insert poppy seedpods at staggered heights near center of arrangement.
6. Arrange 4 popcorn branches among poppy seedpods, reserving the 2 shortest branches for later use.
7. Place large sunflower and protea at base of rocks; insert small sunflower above and to the left.
8. Fill any openings in design with cotton-boll branches and 2 remaining popcorn branches.

SPIRIT OF THE HARVEST

Golden yellow and burnished orange blossoms evoke the spirit of the harvest. This handsome twig planter sits atop an antique plow in a hay field on a farm. The rustic arrangement would look equally charming on a dry sink in a country kitchen or on a table in a sunroom.

Materials

Wooden twig planter, 32 inches long by 5 inches wide

Sheet moss

6 blocks florist's foam

19-gauge florist's wire

Green floral tape

1 long, green, wired pick

3 curly willow branches (available at florist shops)

SILICA-DRIED FLOWERS:

12 sunflowers, ranging in color from light to dark yellow

6 lilacs

5 Shasta daisies

AIR-DRIED FLOWERS:

4 cattails

3 rose liatris

2 brown dock

8 green hydrangea

6 bunches purple statice (5 or 6 stems per bunch)

18 large yellow strawflowers

9 yellow craspedia

Instructions

1. Line the open twig planter with sheet moss and fill with florist's foam.
2. Grasping the stems in the palm of your hand, make a loose bouquet of the cattails, liatris, and dock. Attach the gathered stems to the wired pick and cover pick and stems where they are joined with floral tape. Place upright in left side of planter.
3. Using 19-gauge wire and floral tape, wire stems for the silica-dried flowers.
4. Position sunflowers in florist's foam, with larger flowers near front edge of planter (refer to photograph for placement).
5. Add hydrangea and purple statice, inserting some at an angle so that they extend over front edge of planter.
6. Place lilacs towards front right end of planter.
7. Insert Shasta daisies around lilacs.
8. Add strawflowers and craspedia throughout.
9. Insert curly willow branches into left end of planter.

BERIBBONED STRAWFLOWER WREATH

This welcoming wreath can be hung inside the house, or on an outside door that's protected by a mesh, plastic, or glass screen. If the wreath is hung outside, apply several coats of clear acrylic or hair spray to prevent the dried flowers from absorbing moisture.

Materials

18-inch Styrofoam or straw wreath

Sheet moss

Hairpin hooks

19-gauge florist's wire

Green floral tape

1½ yards two-inch-wide wired-ribbon

1 floral pick

3 beech branches, glycerinized

5 'Teddy Bear' sunflowers, silica-dried

AIR-DRIED FLOWERS:

24 yellow strawflowers

24 white strawflowers

3 bittersweet stems

6 Chinese lantern stems

5 rosy beige hydrangea

3 green hop flowers

Instructions

1. Cover wreath with sheet moss using hairpin hooks (for instructions on how to make hooks, see page 200).

2. Using a total of 36 strawflowers, evenly space four double rows, each consisiting of one band yellow and one band white blooms, on right side of wreath. (Refer to photograph for placement.)

3. Using 19-gauge wire and floral tape, wire beech branches, bittersweet, and Chinese lantern, and secure onto left side of wreath, positioning in a sweeping curve.

4. Tie a bow from the wired-ribbon, attach to floral pick, and insert on left side of wreath.

5. Wire sunflowers, and add the 2 largest to the center-left as focal points.

6. Fill in bare spaces with remaining sunflowers, and add hydrangea and hop flowers.

7. Scatter the remaining 12 strawflowers throughout the design, to soften the borders of the center-left cluster of flowers.

RUSTIC FALL ARRANGEMENT

A graceful design of bittersweet vines, mountain ash branches, and Chinese lanterns decorates a wooden watering can. An antique wooden bucket or a brown-glazed crock would be an equally effective country-style container.

Materials

Wooden watering can

1 block florist's foam

3 long picks

3 pomegranates, fresh

6 bittersweet vines, fresh

8 Chinese lantern stems, air-dried

7 mountain ash branches, glycerinized

Instructions

1. Fit florist's foam securely into watering can.
2. Form outline of design with mountain ash branches.
3. Attach fresh pomegranates to long picks and add near center of arrangement. They will air-dry on picks.
4. Open 1 Chinese lantern blossom into a full-faced flower (for instructions, see page 46), and position in center of arrangement; surround with remaining Chinese lanterns.
5. Remove leaves from 5 bittersweet vines, and insert so that they shoot up and outward.
6. Drape remaining bittersweet vine (with leaves) at base of watering can. Bittersweet will air-dry in position.

THE CARDINAL WREATH

Decorative red cardinals sing from the branches of bright white birch on this rustic wreath. Formed from found pieces of tree bark, and easily assembled using a hot-glue gun, it makes a wonderful holiday gift. Hung from the front door, it's also a cheerful way to welcome guests.

18-inch-diameter Styrofoam wreath

Sheet moss

Hairpin hooks

Hot-glue gun and glue sticks

19-gauge florist's wire

Green floral tape

1½ yards red roping

1 wired pick

2 wired red cardinal ornaments (available at craft and florist shops)

12 to 15 pieces of fallen or loose bark from hickory or birch trees

3 clusters of white ammobium (3 to 4 stems per cluster), air-dried

3 white birch branches

Instructions

1. Cover wreath with sheet moss, using small hairpin hooks (for instructions on how to make hooks, see page 200).
2. Using hot-glue gun, attach bark pieces to sheet moss, following the circular form of the wreath.
3. Wire and tape small clusters of ammobium and insert in the spaces between the bark pieces.
4. Using hot-glue gun, attach white birch branches to bottom of wreath, just off-center (refer to photograph for placement).
5. Position red cardinal ornaments, one at the top of the wreath, the other at the base of the birch branches.
6. Tie a bow from the red roping, attach it to wired pick, and insert at bottom of wreath, beneath cardinal ornament.

Chapter Nine

THE COUNTRY LOOK

There is a garden in childhood,
An enchanted place where
colors are brighter,
The air softer, and the morning
More fragrant than ever before.

ELIZABETH LAWRENCE

SIMPLICITY AND PRACTICALITY were the hallmarks of colonial life. It's easy to romanticize the period, but in reality early American settlers were concerned with survival. Flowers were not grown for pleasure. Plants—mostly herbs—were grown in small kitchen gardens for culinary and medicinal purposes. Some were added as seasoning to food, and others, such as tansy, were applied as insect repellent. Even the lowly goldenrod served a function for the colonists: Its flower heads were boiled to obtain a yellow dye. Decorative bouquets consisted of wildflowers such as Queen Anne's lace, gathered from open fields and placed at random in an old tin cup, a glazed crock, or a firkin. Colors were subdued and neutral. It's this naturalistic, somewhat stark feeling that characterizes country-style dried flower arrangements. Compared to strictly structured Victorian bouquets, country designs emphasize the inherent unpredictability of the elements.

The 200-year-old Miller farm, once a stagecoach stop and inn, is now home to hundreds of flowers, housed in everything from window boxes to antique carts.

COLONIAL WILLIAMSBURG ⚘ Gardening and flower arranging changed dramatically after the English settled and prospered in Williamsburg, Virginia (1699–1780). Society's upper classes beautified their homes year-round with floral arrangements, and the art of drying flowers flourished. Orchards and fields reflected the availability of new flower varieties, including roses, tulips, and violets brought over by Dutch colonists, and carnations, chrysanthemums, dahlias, foxgloves, gladioli, lilies, and strawflowers from England. Thomas Jefferson (1743–1826) lined his garden paths with globe amaranth, his favorite everlasting. On his desk he would place a casual winter bouquet of dried blossoms.

By the nineteenth century, gardening had taken root in American households. Acroclinium, ammobium, gomphrena, helichrysum, rhodanthe, and xeranthemum were just a few of the everlastings listed in the 1891 catalog of Eastman's in Maine.

THE STORY OF A COLONIAL FARM ⚘ Twenty years ago my husband and I bought an old, colonial, country home in upstate New York, where I now grow all my flowers. Built before 1761 in the federal style, it has a central beehive chimney, a hand-pegged roof, five fireplaces, and a smokehouse in the attic chimney. While restoring it, we uncovered a kitchen fireplace complete with the original brick floor, limestone slab sides, and a crane hung with blackened cooking pots. We later learned that the farmhouse had served as an inn and a stagecoach stop. If I close my eyes, I can imagine the quantities of herbs and flowers hung above this fireplace in those busy days.

While digging to establish flower beds, we found more evidence of the farm's interesting past—hundreds of inkwells, medicine bottles, flasks, flow-blue antique pottery, and broken dishes, crocks, and vases. Some of these items were probably used to hold a posy or two in their day. Lilac bushes and a few dark red peony plants were all that remained of a cutting garden. (Coincidentally, these are my two very favorite flowers to dry—both keep well after being preserved in silica gel.) Over the years, many new "patches of color" have been added in every direction around these two remnants of a bygone garden.

FRUITS, FLOWERS, AND HERBS ⚘ Many of the same herbs used in colonial days—chives, oregano, sage, and tansy—are now inserted as pretty accents in dried arrangements. Goldenrod works well as filler material, and Queen Anne's lace adds a wonderfully airy touch to a country design. The early settlers strung apple and citrus slices to dry by the fireplace. Today, the selection of fruits for drying is limitless. When incorporated into seasonal designs, fruit brings a certain freshness and cheer—what better way to express nature's abundance at Thanksgiving than with apples, oranges, and pears?

Every country kitchen could benefit from a box of honesty. Also known as money plant, it air-dries in 2 weeks.

BIRCH BASKET

This unique country-style arrangement combines fresh birch branches with dried honesty. Honesty is also known as money plant, due to its circular seedpods: When rubbed gently, they reveal a shiny disc similar to a silver coin. Any variety of branches—dogwood, cherry, blackberry—could be used in place of the birch.

Materials

Vertical birch basket

Cylindrical vase

1 block florist's foam, broken into small pieces

8 birch branches, fresh

10 stems honesty, of varying sizes, air-dried

Instructions

1. Place vase inside basket and fill with water.
2. Stuff pieces of dry florist's foam between vase and basket, leaving a 2-inch-wide piece extended about 1 inch above front rim of vase.
3. Cut fresh birch branches and hammer cut ends to facilitate water uptake. Place in vase, with highest branches at center of arrangement.
4. Insert 7 long stems of honesty into florist's foam, keeping design airy and basket handle exposed.
5. Insert remaining short stems of honesty into extended piece of florist's foam at front of vase, so that they cascade over rim.
6. Add water to vase every few days as needed.

THE FLOWERING BIRDCAGE

Any bird would sing at the sight of cheerful strawflowers, golden yarrow, green hop vines, and frothy Ming fern fronds. Unusual containers, such as antique birdcages or colored-glass flasks, lend themselves to quaint country arrangements. My husband and I found these bottles and jars on the farm when we were first breaking ground for my flower gardens.

Materials

Antique or ornate birdcage

2-inch square of Styrofoam

Sheet moss

Hot-glue gun and glue sticks

Hairpin hooks

1 decorative bird ornament

2 Ming fern fronds, glycerinized

2 hop vines, air-dried

3 short stems gold yarrow, air-dried

4 red strawflowers, air-dried

4 pink strawflowers, air-dried

Instructions

1. Cover Styrofoam square with sheet moss, using hairpin hooks to secure in place (for instructions on how to make hooks, see page 200).

2. Using hot-glue gun, attach Styrofoam square to the floor of the birdcage, just left of the cage door. Allow to dry.

3. Hot-glue bird ornament to hanger: Position to the right of the Styrofoam square.

4. Insert cascading Ming fern fronds and hop vines into Styrofoam square (refer to photograph for placement).

5. Add yarrow toward top of arrangement.

6. Scatter strawflowers throughout arrangement, with larger flowers near open door of cage.

WINDBLOWN WREATH

The wild heart of the country is captured in this windblown wreath. It requires very few dried flowers: Its beauty lies in the graceful lines of the bare branches. Here, fresh white willow stems are twisted into shape, but a similar effect can be achieved with any type of flexible branch or vine, such as bittersweet or wild grape, stripped of leaves.

Materials

Dark green floral tape

19-gauge florist's wire

Spool-wire

8 to 10 white willow branches, fresh

3 eucalyptus stems, glycerinized

SILICA-DRIED FLOWERS:

2 purple coneflowers

2 Queen Anne's lace

AIR-DRIED FLOWERS:

4 pink astilbe

2 white larkspur

2 purple larkspur

2 pink larkspur

3 short stems purple statice

3 short stems pink statice

Instructions

1. In early spring, gather thin, supple, white willow branches and twist them into a swirling, airy wreath about 12 inches in diameter. Allow many "spokes" to shoot out from the body of the wreath. Use spool-wire to bind branches together. The wreath will air-dry in position in 3 weeks, and can be decorated anytime afterwards.

2. Using 19-gauge wire and floral tape, wire stems for the eucalyptus, astilbe, statice, coneflowers, and Queen Anne's lace.

3. Insert eucalyptus stems into twists of wreath so that branches fan out from three equidistant points on arrangement.

4. Tuck in 2 astilbe at top of wreath and 2 at bottom.

5. Repeat with larkspur, using 2 groups of 3 colors each.

6. Tape all 6 stems of statice together and insert bunch at center left side of wreath.

7. Add coneflowers and Queen Anne's lace as accents to complete the design.

THE SITTING DUCK

Whether nesting within a chickweed table wreath or nestled in a bookshelf niche, this decorated duck will make himself at home in almost any corner of the house. A pair, used to flank a mantelpiece, adds an outdoorsy accent to a country cabin or hunting lodge. The recipe for the wreath is on the following page.

Materials

Plastic or wooden duck

Sheet moss

Hot-glue gun with glue sticks

½ yard one-inch-wide green
   wired-ribbon

Green floral tape

Spool-wire

1 small wired pick

13 small lemon leaves,
   glycerinized

1 yellow strawflower, air-dried

2 stems white pearly
   everlasting, air-dried

1 nigella (love-in-a-mist)
   seedpod, air-dried

1 stem bittersweet, air-dried

Instructions

1. Using hot-glue gun, cover duck's body with sheet moss; leave head exposed.

2. Using hot-glue gun, attach lemon leaves, reverse side exposed, in overlapping rows of 3 across duck's back, to form "feathers." Add 1 leaf to tail end.

3. Make a bow from wired-ribbon and tie around duck's neck.

4. Using spool-wire and floral tape, bunch the strawflower, pearly everlasting, nigella seedpod, and bittersweet into a small bouquet, attach to wired pick, and cover stems and pick with floral tape.

5. Insert bouquet under bow at duck's neck.

CHICKWEED TABLE WREATH

Weeds and wild grasses make for unusual backgrounds in country-style and casual arrangements. Pick the stems in the early green stages for the most vibrant color when dried. Because the material shrinks slightly as it dries, be sure to have a generous supply on hand.

Materials

16-inch diameter double-wire wreath frame

Spool-wire

Floral tape

Stems of chickweed (fresh or air-dried, an armful should do)

8 artichokes, air-dried and attached to green picks (see page 200)

6 bunches white pearly everlasting (5 stems per bunch), air-dried

7 golden yellow tansy flowers, air-dried

20 nigella (love-in-a-mist) seedpods, air-dried

Instructions

1. Using spool-wire, group short stems of chickweed together into bunches: Cover wired stems with floral tape.

2. Generously layer chickweed bunches around wreath frame.

3. Insert artichokes into wreath; space evenly.

4. Group pearly everlasting bunches, tansy flowers, and nigella seedpods into 8 assorted bunches. Not every bunch will contain pearly everlasting or tansies. Insert 1 near each artichoke.

5. Set THE SITTING DUCK (see page 140) in center of table wreath, if desired.

BOUNTIFUL MANTEL PIECE

An abundance of roses, yarrow, and cockscomb cascade over the edges of a mantel. The profusion of flowers is sure to warm up a room, whether or not there's a fire in the hearth.

Materials

1 piece chicken wire, trimmed to the length of the mantel

10 blocks florist's foam

19-gauge florist's wire

Green floral tape

Sheet moss

Hairpin hooks

2 pewter candlesticks

2 candles

22 lemon leaves, glycerinized

SILICA-DRIED FLOWERS:

3 pink peonies

2 red peonies

4 white peonies

3 maroon zinnias

2 pink zinnias

2 purple zinnias

11 pink 'Queen Elizabeth' roses

1 white 'Casablanca' lily

1 lavender hydrangea

AIR-DRIED FLOWERS:

16 strawflowers, assorted white and pink

12 maroon crested cockscomb

8 gold yarrow

14 green hydrangea

9 hop vines, with flowers

10 bunches lady's mantle

Instructions

1. Roll chicken wire around blocks of florist's foam and secure with 19-gauge wire.

2. Cover chicken-wired foam block with sheet moss, using hairpin hooks to secure (for instructions on how to make hooks, see page 200). Set on mantel.

3. Cut openings through the wire at the right corner and insert candlesticks with candles.

4. Using 19-gauge wire and floral tape, wire stems for lemon leaves and silica-dried flowers.

5. Insert lemon leaves as background along the top, bottom, and ends of foam block.

6. Insert cockscomb along length of mantel; scatter peonies and zinnias above.

7. Insert yarrow at rear of arrangement, above peonies and zinnias.

8. Use lady's mantle and hydrangea to fill large empty spaces.

9. Place lily in center of arrangement.

10. Scatter roses and strawflowers throughout.

11. Insert hop vines so that they cascade out and over front of arrangement.

BOUQUET IN A GILDED FRAME

Wherever you hang this pretty picture, it will be a charming accessory. The selection of flowers can be personalized according to individual taste or interior design, and the finished picture hung on a door to designate a particular room. To secure the small florets and sectioned blossoms, each flower is reinforced with dabs of clear-drying glue.

Materials

Oval convex frame

½ yard off-white felt

Clear-drying glue such as Sobo (available at craft stores)

19-gauge wire

Green floral tape

1 fern frond, pressed or glycerinized , cut into small sections

AIR-DRIED FLOWERS:

6 larkspur stems, blossoms removed

7 pink larkspur

3 golden yarrow

4 blue delphinium florets

3 white pearly everlasting

2 blue globe thistle

4 purple statice

SILICA-DRIED FLOWERS:

3 dark pink zinnias

4 light pink roses

1 blue hydrangea, broken into small sections

3 pink pompon dahlias

2 Shasta daisies

4 white feverfew

Instructions

1. Trace frame on a piece of plain paper. Using outline as a guide, trim felt in an oval shape slightly large than the frame itself. Glue felt to frame backing, wrapping any excess over the edges.

2. Glue larkspur stems to felt backing, to form base of bouquet.

3. Using just a dab of glue, place small sections of fern on felt backing, in a fanlike shape.

4. Define outer edges of design with pink larkspur.

5. Using 19-gauge wire and floral tape, wire short stems for the silica-dried flowers.

6. Add zinnias at base of design, on top of larkspur stems.

7. Place roses above zinnias.

8. Fill out design with hydrangea sections, dahlias, daisies, and yarrow.

9. Add delphinium, pearly everlasting, globe thistle, feverfew, and statice in any open spaces between the larger flowers.

PRETTY PINKS AND BLUES

The spiked blossoms of artemisia, liatris, and larkspur spread out like feathers from this fan-shaped vase, giving the arrangement a wonderful, wide-open feeling, while the full, rounded flower heads of roses and peonies add warmth to the design.

Materials

Pink, fan-shaped vase
1 block florist's foam
19-gauge florist's wire
Green floral tape

AIR-DRIED FLOWERS:
10 'Silver King' artemisia
5 rose liatris
8 pink larkspur
8 blue larkspur

3 red crested cockscomb
3 blue hydrangea
5 purple statice stems
5 white strawflowers
5 pink strawflowers
6 white acroclinium

SILICA-DRIED FLOWERS:
5 pink peonies
6 pink roses

Instructions

1. Secure florist's foam in center of vase, leaving 2 inches extended above rim.
2. Establish the overall size of the design by inserting, in order, artemisia, liatris, pink larkspur, and blue larkspur. Arrange the flowers in a fan-shape that mimics the configuration of the vase.
3. Using 19-gauge wire and floral tape, wire stems for the silica-dried flowers.
4. Starting at the base and working upward, add cockscomb and peonies so that florist's foam is concealed from view.
5. Insert roses (refer to photograph on page 147 for placement).
6. Fill in bare or sparse spaces with, in order, hydrangea, statice, strawflowers, and acroclinium.

FIVE-FINGER DESIGN

The typical blue-and-white "finger" vase featured on the following page is as popular today as it was during the Williamsburg era. In fact, I had the pleasure of creating such an arrangement for the White House during the Reagan administration. Long, spikey blossoms of larkspur, delphinium, artemisia, and lavender form fitting floral "fingers" for the vase.

Materials

Williamsburg-style finger vase
Sand or pebbles
1 block florist's foam
19-gauge floral wire
Green floral tape

GLYCERINIZED MATERIAL:
9 magnolia leaves
5 baby's breath

AIR-DRIED FLOWERS:
12 pink larkspur
6 blue delphinium
9 'Silver King' artemisia

20 lavender
8 white strawflowers
8 pink strawflowers
3 blue globe thistle

SILICA-DRIED FLOWERS:
5 pink 'Queen Elizabeth' roses
4 light blue hydrangea
2 white 'Peter Pan' zinnias
2 pale pink 'Peter Pan' zinnias
2 deep pink 'Peter Pan' zinnias
3 purple asters
2 deep pink pompon dahlias

Instructions

1. Fill bottom of vase with sand or pebbles, for stability.
2. Cut florist's foam into 5 narrow sections, each 4 inches long: Push 1 piece into each "finger," leaving 1 inch of foam extended above each opening.
3. Using 19-gauge wire and floral tape, wire stems for the magnolia leaves and silica-dried flowers.
4. Insert magnolia leaves at the back of each "finger," arching over sides of vase.
5. Add larkspur, delphinium, artemisia, and bunches of lavender (3 to 5 stems per bunch) in front of magnolia leaves.
6. Insert roses as focal flowers, one in each "finger," at base of arrangement.
7. Place hydrangeas and zinnias to the left and right of roses, near bottom half of arrangement.
8. Scatter asters and dahlias above hydrangeas and zinnias.
9. Fill in any small open spaces with strawflowers.
10. Add touches of globe thistle and stems of baby's breath for an airy effect.

BUSH WHITE HOUSE ARRANGEMENT

The delphinium and hydrangea in this arrangement match the container and are in keeping with Barbara Bush's love of blue. Soft colors complete the elegant design, which the former First Lady found "unbelievably beautiful."

Materials

Blue vase

2 blocks florist's foam

19-gauge florist's wire

Green floral tape

9 lemon leaves with stems, glycerinized

AIR-DRIED FLOWERS:

15 'Silver King' artemisia

12 pink statice

2 pink 'Floradale' crested cockscomb

7 pink strawflowers

SILICA-DRIED FLOWERS:

7 blue delphinium

5 pink larkspur

4 blue hydrangea

10 'Pink Fantastic' zinnias

4 white peonies

3 'Heart's Delight' (bicolor) roses

Instructions

1. Fill vase with florist's foam, leaving 2 inches extended above rim.
2. Using 19-gauge wire and floral tape, wire long stems for the lemon leaves, artemisia, and silica-dried flowers.
3. Establish height, width, and general outline of design with lemon leaves.
4. Insert artemisia, delphinium, and larkspur in front of and following outline of lemon leaves.
5. Use pink statice to fill in any spaces around already inserted materials.
6. Position hydrangea as focal points in arrangement.
7. Set cockscomb near center of arrangement, one almost on top of the other.
8. Scatter zinnias throughout, with largest blossoms near bottom of arrangement.
9. Surround cockscomb with peonies.
10. Situate roses in center of arrangement.
11. Fill in any bare spots with strawflowers.

ANTIQUE PITCHER ARRANGEMENT

Picture this water pitcher on a dry sink, a marble-top table, or even a windowsill above a porcelain bathtub. The deep red of the cockscomb and rich purple of the larkspur, delphinium, and lilac are intensified by the clean white container.

Materials

Antique water pitcher

1 block florist's foam

19-gauge florist's wire

Green floral tape

1 bunch decorative grapes

10 sprengeri fern stems, glycerinized and dyed green (see Chapter 6)

SILICA-DRIED FLOWERS:

8 white peonies

6 lilacs

AIR-DRIED FLOWERS:

7 rose liatris

7 purple larkspur

5 dark purple delphinium

5 large maroon crested cockscomb

7 gold yarrow

Instructions

1. Fix florist's foam securely in pitcher, leaving 2 inches extended above rim.
2. Using 19-gauge wire and floral tape, wire stems for the silica-dried flowers.
3. Form outline of design with liatris, larkspur, and delphinium.
4. Place 3 large cockscomb at base of design: Stagger the other 2 above them.
5. Surround cockscomb with 6 peonies.
6. Further define outline of design by adding lilacs alongside liatris, larkspur, and delphinium.
7. Fill in empty spaces with 6 yarrow.
8. Add fern stems for an airy effect.
9. To accessorize, place decorative grapes on the table to the right of the pitcher's handle. Insert the remaining peonies and yarrow into the grapes for an added touch.

AROMATIC ORANGE TREE

Few fragrances are as evocative as clove-oranges. The combination of fresh citrus and clove spice brings to mind cold winter nights, hot mugs of tea, warm flannel blankets, and roaring fireplaces. Aromatic Orange Trees make decorative dining room ornaments from early fall to Thanksgiving. For variety, substitute lemons, limes, or apples for oranges, and use groupings of nuts or cellophane-wrapped candies in place of grapes.

Materials

Wooden, nail-studded cone

12-inch-diameter circle of thick corrugated cardboard

1 roll clear, wide mailing tape

15 small wired picks

36 boxwood clippings

28 oranges, various sizes

1 can whole cloves

1 large bunch green grapes

16 magnolia leaves, glycerinized

16 yellow strawflowers, air-dried

Instructions

1. Place cone on cardboard base.
2. Cover edge of cardboard base by alternating magnolia leaves and boxwood clippings in a circular pattern, securing each with tape.
3. Stud a few of the oranges with cloves, arranging them in different patterns for variety: Puncture the orange peels with a needle first, then insert ends of cloves. Some juice will run out of the oranges in the process, so cover the work surface with paper towels or work over a sink.
4. Spike oranges onto cone, starting with the largest fruit at the base and working upward with the smaller ones.
5. Wedge sprigs of boxwood in between the oranges.
6. Wire small bunches of grapes to picks and scatter throughout arrangement.
7. Insert strawflowers at random for additional color.

Chapter Ten

HOLIDAY DESIGNS

Flowers...

They spring to cheer the sense
and glad the heart.

ANNA LETITIA BARBAULD

HOLIDAYS OFFER THE PERFECT excuse for all kinds of elaborate projects. The traditional symbols and colors associated with each occasion offer loose guidelines for thematic dried flower designs. Starting with a simple Easter lily or classic Christmas ornament as a focal point, arrangements can be expanded to include just about any item that brings to mind the day at hand: Champagne flutes for New Year's Eve; American flags on the Fourth of July; painted pumpkins for Halloween. The object is to have fun.

The arrangements featured in this chapter commemorate major holidays, but it's equally important to acknowledge personal milestones. Incorporate a child's favorite flowers into a birthday bouquet. Frame a diploma with pressed olive leaves and gold sheaths of wheat. Fill a home office with money plant for success and shamrocks for good luck. When created with a little imagination, holiday arrangements can add real meaning to a room.

With its seasonal shades of green and gold, this berried bittersweet wreath welcomes weary trick-or-treaters. An abundance of pumpkins and buckets of mums complete the Halloween scene.

HAPPY NEW YEAR ARRANGEMENT

Light two candles at the stroke of midnight: one for the year gone by, one for the year to come. A silver candelabrum brings elegance and a certain dignity to any New Year celebration, white chrysanthemums offer joy, and red roses speak of love. With ripe pyracantha berries, curly willow branches, and frothy asparagus ferns, this sweeping arrangement bursts with the promise of new beginnings.

Materials

3-armed silver candelabrum

1 can silver spray-paint

1 candle adapter with three-inch-round block of florist's foam (available at craft and floral shops)

2 red candles, each 18 inches long

19-gauge florist's wire

Green floral tape

8 silver curly willow branches (available at craft and floral shops during the holiday season, or you can spray-paint your own)

5 caspia branches, air-dried

3 red-berried pyracantha sprays, glycerinized

6 asparagus fern branches, glycerinized

12 red 'Mercedes' roses, silica-dried

3 white chrysanthemums, silica-dried

Instructions

1. Spray caspia branches with silver spray-paint, following manufacturer's directions. Let dry.

2. Insert candle adapter, filled with 3-inch-round block of florist's foam, into center arm of candelabrum.

3. Insert caspia and asparagus ferns into florist's foam so that they form an "S" curve.

4. Using 19-gauge florist's wire and tape, wire roses and chrysanthemums: Insert roses into florist's foam, following the line of the "S" curve. Cluster larger and more open roses in center of arrangement.

5. Add chrysanthemums above and below the center roses, for contrast.

6. Insert pyracantha sprays near center flowers as background filler.

7. Use silver curly willow branches to further enhance the "S" curve, leaving a few projecting outward from the front of the design.

8. Put candles in left and right arms of candelabrum. (Never leave lighted candles unattended, especially when they are in the midst of an arrangement, dried or fresh.)

VALENTINE'S DAY WREATH

Valentine's Day is a sentimental occasion for young and old alike. Nothing expresses love quite like roses—except maybe a luscious box of chocolates! On this enchanting floral wreath, the ribbon-wrapped hearts signify "two in love." White 'President Kennedy' roses woo delicate pink 'Delores' blooms, and both are bedded in feathery clouds of baby's breath. As a testament to the enduring nature of true love, the wreath can be left up year-round.

Materials

16-inch-diameter, heart-shaped
  Styrofoam wreath

Sheet moss

Hairpin hooks

Craft glue (such as Sobo)

19-gauge florist's wire

Green floral tape

2 small, wired Styrofoam hearts
  (available at craft stores)

2 yards floral-patterned ribbon

2 wired picks

13 maidenhair fern pieces,
  glycerinized

30 baby's breath stems,
  glycerinized

13 pink 'Delores' roses,
  silica-dried

13 white 'President Kennedy'
  roses, silica-dried

2 rosebuds, silica-dried

Instructions

1. Cover wreath with sheet moss, securing with hairpin hooks (for instructions on how to make hooks, see page 200).

2. Frame edge of wreath with maidenhair fern pieces by pushing them into the Styrofoam.

3. Using 19-gauge wire and floral tape, wire roses and rosebuds and insert in a crescent shape along left side of wreath, placing buds along outer edge (refer to photograph for placement).

4. Using 19-gauge wire and floral tape, wire clusters of baby's breath and insert between roses to create a soft background.

5. Wrap small Styrofoam hearts with ribbon. Each heart takes about ½ yard of ribbon. Put a dab of craft glue at one end of the ribbon piece, attach to heart, then, holding glued end in place with one hand, tightly wind ribbon around heart form with the other. Secure tail end of ribbon with another dab of glue.

6. Using the remaining yard of ribbon, tie 2 bows, and wire to picks.

7. Attach ribbon-covered hearts to right side of wreath, and insert bows beneath them.

ST. PATRICK'S DAY BOWL

Irish eyes will be smiling at the sight of this unusual combination of fresh and dried materials—including full heads of cabbage more commonly seen alongside the corned beef! On St. Patrick's, "the wearing o' the green" is the order o' the day, so it's fitting that the different colors of the ivy, grapes, apples, peppers, and zinnias bring to mind "the old sod."

Materials

Large, deep, oval pottery bowl

Hot-glue gun and glue sticks

Floral putty

19-gauge florist's wire

Green floral tape

2 blocks florist's foam

1 long wired pick

15 long picks or skewers

5 dogwood branches, each about 25 inches long, with corresponding silica-dried dogwood blossoms

5 'Envy' zinnias, silica-dried

5 bells of Ireland, silica-dried

3 heads cabbage: 2 regular, 1 Savoy, fresh

6-inch pot of ivy, fresh

1 large bunch green grapes, fresh

8 Granny Smith apples, fresh

6 long Italian, or frying, green peppers, fresh

1 leek, fresh

Instructions

1. Use hot-glue gun to attach silica-dried dogwood blossoms to branches. Set aside to dry.

2. Secure florist's foam in base of bowl with floral putty.

3. Skewer cabbages with picks, and place on top of foam, leaving room in the center for the pot of ivy. Gently open outer leaves so that they extend over edge of bowl.

4. Center pot of ivy among cabbage heads and let vines trail over edge of bowl.

5. Attach bunch of grapes to wired pick, wrapping wire securely around grape stems before inserting in front of potted ivy.

6. Insert picks into apples and peppers and position throughout arrangement (refer to photograph for placement).

7. Using 19-gauge wire and floral tape, wire zinnias and insert throughout arrangement.

8. Using 19-gauge wire and floral tape, wire bells of Ireland and insert along with leeks into foam at rear of arrangement, for added height and variety of color.

9. Add dogwood branches to outer edges of arrangement.

EASTER BUNNY BASKET

A wicker basket, filled with lilies and graced by none other than the Easter bunny himself, celebrates both the sacred and secular aspects of the holiday.

Materials

10-x-14-inch wicker basket

Rectangular cookie tin, sized to line wicker basket

6 blocks florist's foam

Hot-glue gun and glue sticks

2 wooden picks

19-gauge florist's wire

Dark green floral tape

Sheet moss

Spanish moss

Hairpin hooks

6-inch-tall stuffed bunny

6 chocolate Easter eggs

4-inch pot of ivy

4-inch pot of lavender African violet

6 purple statice, air-dried

2 green hydrangea, broken into pieces, air-dried

2 bunches green bunny's-tail grass, air-dried

3 stems sea lavender, air-dried

3 stems lady's mantle, air-dried

12 miniature 'Tête à Tête' daffodils, silica-dried

4 yellow lilies, silica-dried

6 green-dyed palm fronds, each at least 2 feet tall, glycerinized

Instructions

1. Line wicker basket with cookie tin and fill with florist's foam.
2. Carve out 2 openings in left side of foam: one for the pot of ivy, the other, slightly to the right, for the pot of African violet. Set plants in foam.
3. Cover interior of basket, including pots, with sheet moss. Secure with hairpin hooks (for instructions on how to make hooks, see page 200).
4. Using hot-glue gun, dot glue along outer edge of basket and cover with Spanish moss.
5. Using 19-gauge wire and floral tape, wire stems for the daffodils and lilies.
6. Glue florets of statice, pieces of hydrangea, and miniature daffodils to Spanish moss.
7. Tape each bunch of bunny's-tail grass to a wooden pick and insert into foam behind ivy.
8. Add sea lavender and lady's mantle among the bunny's-tail grass.
9. Place bunny at right rear side of basket, and scatter chocolate Easter eggs around him.
10. Leaving approximately 5-inch stems for eventual insertion into foam, bend tops of 3 palm fronds into 4- to 5-inch circles, using hot-glue gun to secure.
11. Insert largest frond circle at left rear of arrangement, second at back center, alongside the bunny, and third over front right edge of basket (refer to photograph for placement).
12. Add remaining palm fronds to rear of arrangement.
13. Position lilies across front of arrangement: 2 facing forward alongside the bunny, 2 standing upright, centered in front of palm fronds and bunny's-tail grass.

MOTHER'S DAY HATBOX

The accompanying hatbox arrangement, filled with whimsical zinnias, delicate fronds of larkspur, and tender tea roses, is exquisitely feminine. Hatbox reproductions are readily available today, but an old jewelry box with lid raised or a small antique storage chest makes an equally handsome container.

Materials

8-inch-diameter hatbox with floral design

1½ blocks florist's foam

Hot-glue gun and glue sticks

19-gauge florist's wire

Green floral tape

10 lemon leaves, glycerinized

AIR-DRIED FLOWERS:

6 pink larkspur

2 pink crested cockscomb

3 pink strawflowers

7 baby's-breath stems

SILICA-DRIED FLOWERS:

6 hybrid tea roses: 3 white 'President Kennedy' and 3 bicolor 'Heart's Delight,' silica-dried

3 pink 'Peter Pan' zinnias

2 dark pink asters

2 purple coneflowers

3 pink 'The Fairy' roses

6 pale pink Japanese anemones with buds

14 white feverfew stems

Instructions

1. Fill bottom of hatbox with florist's foam, leaving 2 inches extended above rim.
2. Prop box top at an angle against rear of box bottom, and, using hot-glue gun, attach to florist's foam.
3. Using 19-gauge wire and floral tape, wire lemon leaves and silica-dried flowers.
4. Insert lemon leaves along edges of florist's foam.
5. Insert larkspur stems so that they extend horizontally from edges of box.
6. Position tea roses at base and middle of arrangement, as focal points.
7. Surround roses with cockscomb and zinnias.
8. Add asters and coneflowers to each end of box.
9. Fill in sparse spots with 'The Fairy' roses, Japanese anemone, feverfew, strawflowers, and baby's breath.

MOTHER'S DAY TUSSIE-MUSSIE

Tussie-mussies—those sweet, circular nosegays so popular with Victorian ladies—can still deliver secret messages on special occasions. In the language of flowers, baby's breath recognizes a pure heart, pink roses symbolize grace, and fern fronds signify sincerity. On Mother's Day, profess your devotion with this demure expression of love.

Materials

Filigree posy holder

4-inch-square piece of lace

Hot-glue gun and glue sticks

19-gauge florist's wire

Dark green floral tape

1-x-3-inch piece of florist's foam

5 Australian daisy stems (available at florist shops)

5 fern tips, each about 2 to 3 inches long, glycerinized

1 small pink crested cockscomb, air-dried

5 baby's breath stems, air-dried

7 miniature pink 'Cupcake' roses, silica-dried

1 miniature rosebud, silcia-dried

Instructions

1. Using hot-glue gun, attach lace square to posy holder and fan out edges.
2. Push piece of florist's foam over lace into holder.
3. Using 19-gauge wire and floral tape, wire short stems for the fern tips, cockscomb, baby's breath, roses, and rosebud.
4. Insert fern tips all around outer edge of florist's foam.
5. Insert cockscomb in center of florist's foam.
6. Insert roses toward center of arrangement, extend bud out toward edge.
7. Insert baby's breath along with Australian daisies throughout arrangement.
8. Position in front of the MOTHER'S DAY HATBOX shown on page 169.

FATHER'S DAY TRIBUTE

To remind dad of the great outdoors, this Father's Day arrangement includes branches of silver-dollar eucalyptus and berry-covered mountain ash, along with sunflowers, black-eyed Susans, even orange slices. I used one of my father's favorite pewter mugs to set the tone for the design, then accessorized it with items pleasing to him—a decanter, brass cordial goblets, and two small books. Familiar objects such as these further personalize an arrangement.

Materials

Large pewter mug and tray

1 block florist's foam

Hot-glue gun and glue sticks

Green floral tape

19-gauge florist's wire

2 picks

5 silver-dollar eucalyptus branches, glycerinized

4 mountain ash branches, each about 8 to 9 inches long, with berries, glycerinized

4 sunflowers, silica-dried

2 black-eyed Susans, silica-dried

7 'Silver King' artemisia, air-dried

5 gold yarrow, air-dried

9 yellow strawflowers, air-dried

7 nigella seedpods, air-dried

2 orange slices, oven-dried

Instructions

1. Trim florist's foam to fit pewter mug, leaving 2 inches extended above rim.
2. Create outline of arrangement by inserting eucalyptus, mountain ash, and artemisia in a sweeping curve from upper left to lower right (refer to photograph on following page for placement).
3. Using 19-gauge wire and floral tape, wire sunflowers and black-eyed Susans.
4. Insert sunflowers toward center of design.
5. Flank sunflowers with black-eyed Susans.
6. Insert yarrow along outer edges of design, and in any large openings.
7. Scatter strawflowers and nigella seedpods throughout.
8. Using hot-glue gun, attach orange slices to picks and insert towards base and top of arrangement (for instructions on how to dry oranges, see page 200).

ANNIVERSARY LOVING CUP

Whether it's one, ten, twenty, or, in my case, forty-five years, a marriage anniversary calls for a special dried-flower design. This loving cup arrangement may call to mind the religious rituals of a wedding ceremony or the celebration that followed afterward—and that romantic first dance as husband and wife.

Materials

Silver or silver-plated
loving cup

1 block florist's foam

19-gauge floral wire

Green floral tape

SILICA-DRIED FLOWERS:

3 red anemones

3 purple anemones

6 pink 'The Fairy' roses

AIR-DRIED FLOWERS:

7 lavender

7 blue salvia

5 pink strawflowers

4 white strawflowers

12 white ammobium

Instructions

1. Trim florist's foam to fit loving cup, leaving 1 inch extended above rim.
2. Create outline of arrangement by inserting lavender and blue salvia.
3. Using 19-gauge wire and floral tape, wire anemones and roses. If necessary, extend wired stems of strawflowers to give them sufficient height in relation to size of loving cup.
4. Insert strawflowers first, anemones next, and roses last (refer to photograph for placement).
5. Using 19-gauge wire and floral tape, wire small bunches of ammobium, and use to fill any empty spaces.

BITTERSWEET HALLOWEEN WREATH

In the wreath shown on page 158, vines of fresh bittersweet, cut just as the berries begin to turn orange, burst into color a few days later. A little extra bittersweet makes a ragged head of hair or a rakish beard for a stylish jack-o'-lantern. Assembly of the wreath is so simple, it's a perfect Halloween activity for the whole family.

Materials

16-inch-diameter double-wire
wreath frame

Fresh bittersweet
Spool-wire

Instructions

1. Cut several long vines of bittersweet just as the orange color is beginning to show in the berries.
2. Wrap bittersweet around wreath frame, securing ends with spool-wire. Fill in face of wreath, weaving vines in and out until frame is completely covered.
3. Hang wreath outdoors: It air-dries naturally, and will burst into color in just a few days.

FRUIT AND FLOWERS

A cornucopia of apples, peppers, and pears makes a memorable Thanksgiving centerpiece. Garnished with wheat and wild rose hips, decorated with a festive pheasant, laden with fresh fruit, this holiday basket holds the abundance of the season. Gather around the table with family and friends, take hands, and give thanks for nature's gifts.

Materials

- 10-x-13-inch wicker basket with handle
- 1 block Styrofoam
- Spool-wire
- Paring knife
- 48 long picks or skewers
- 1 small decorative pheasant on a pick (available at craft and novelty shops)
- 7 beech branches, glycerinized
- 11 green oat stems, air-dried

- 9 wheat stems, air-dried
- 9 rose hip branches, air-dried
- 30 yellow strawflowers, air-dried
- 8 Granny Smith apples
- 10 Gala apples
- 8 Bartlett pears
- 10 Sickle pears
- 3 artichokes
- 2 yellow peppers
- 4 bunches red grapes

Instructions

1. Using spool-wire, attach Styrofoam block to center of open basket.

2. Insert beech branches, green oats, and wheat stems into Styrofoam so that they extend 3 to 4 inches over outer edges of basket (refer to photograph on following page for placement).

3. Attach Granny Smith and Gala apples, Bartlett pears, and artichokes to picks and, working inward from each side of basket, insert in Styrofoam. Leave space in center of basket for eventual placement of grapes.

4. Turn yellow peppers into "tulips": Slice 1½ inches off narrow end and scoop out seeds; with paring knife, cut and shape 7 to 8 "petals." Attach pepper tulips to picks at stem end and insert one on each side of basket.

5. Wire grape bunches to picks and insert in center of arrangement.

6. Attach Sickle pears to picks and use to fill any small openings.

7. Insert strawflowers and rose hip branches throughout arrangement.

8. Add pheasant as a decorative touch.

SANTA IS SURROUNDED

Old St. Nick won't mind the trip down the chimney once he finds himself in this flattering flower wreath, wearing a garland of evergreens and holly berries. Pine cones fill the air with the fresh scent of the season.

30-inch-tall Santa Claus statue

24-inch-diameter spruce wreath (real or artificial)

3 yards of three-inch-wide burgundy wired-ribbon

1 long wired pick

19-gauge florist's wire

Dark green floral tape

Spool-wire

14 pine cones

15 maroon crested cockscomb, air-dried

6 white 'President Kennedy' roses, silica-dried

15 baby's-breath stems, silica-dried

SANTA'S GARLAND:

Hot-glue gun and glue sticks

Small lengths of evergreens

Small stems of holly berries

2 small bicolor 'Fire 'n Ice' rosebuds, silica-dried

1 maroon cockscomb, broken into small sections, air-dried

12 ammobium, air-dried

Instructions

1. Set Santa statue in middle of wreath.

2. Weave ribbon through wreath. Tie a bow from remaining length of ribbon, attach it to wired pick, and insert at right front side of wreath.

3. Using spool-wire, attach pine cones onto wreath in a scattered pattern (for instructions on how to wire pine cones, see page 200).

4. Tuck crested cockscomb throughout arrangement, among pine cones.

5. Using 19-gauge wire and floral tape, wire roses and baby's breath: Attach roses to wreath as focal points; add baby's breath throughout, for an airy, graceful look.

6. To make Santa's garland: Bind small lengths of evergreens together with spool-wire to form a garland; wire rosebuds and hot-glue to garland along with sections of cockscomb and stems of holly berries; hot-glue ammobium among roses and cockscomb. After glue has dried, attach garland to Santa's hands with spool-wire.

CHRISTMAS TREE WREATH

Two symbols of the season are combined in this unusual arrangement: A wreath frames a miniature Christmas tree. The little tree—merry and bright with blossoms of red and white—can stand on its own, but it's much more at home among the branches and pine cones.

Materials

16-inch-diameter grapevine wreath with front pocket (available at garden centers)

10-inch-high Styrofoam cone

2 yards three-inch-wide poinsettia-flowered ribbon

Green sheet moss

Hairpin hooks

19-gauge florist's wire

Dark green floral tape

1 long pick

20 assorted pine cones

24 boxwood branches, glycerinized

30 stems curly parsley, silica-dried

18 red 'Mercedes' roses, silica-dried

16 white strawflowers, air-dried

36 ammobium, air-dried

Instructions

1. Cover Styrofoam cone with sheet moss and secure with hairpin hooks (for instructions on how to make hooks, see page 200).

2. Set cone in open front pocket of grapevine wreath and secure with hairpin hooks.

3. Wire pine cones and attach around base of Styrofoam "tree" and in pocket of wreath (for instructions on how to wire pine cones, see page 200).

4. Wedge clusters of boxwood between pine cones.

5. Using 19-gauge wire and floral tape, wire together clusters of 2 to 3 stems each of curly parsley. Insert into "tree," working from base toward top. Leave openings for roses and strawflowers.

6. Using 19-gauge wire and floral tape, wire roses and attach throughout arrangement, positioning more open blossoms at the middle and bottom of the "tree" (refer to photograph for placement).

7. Wire together small clusters of ammobium, and insert along with strawflowers throughout arrangement to fill any bare spaces.

8. Tie a bow from the ribbon, attach it to pick, and insert on right side of the wreath. Weave ribbon ends loosely through wreath.

FRESH, DRIED, AND SILK

To create charming, long-lasting arrangements, combine fresh, dried, and silk materials. Silk poinsettia blossoms are especially versatile: They can be attached as holiday accents to just about anything—Christmas stockings, window curtains, stair banisters, gift boxes.

Materials

White pedestal urn

1 block florist's foam, soaked in water

1½ yards white wired-ribbon

19-gauge florist's wire

Dark green floral tape

1 wired pick

5 birch branches, spray-painted white (available at florist and craft shops)

3 silk holly branches

3 silk white poinsettias: small, medium, and large

5 white pine branches, fresh

7 boxwood branches, fresh

12 red roses, silica-dried

Instructions

1. Fill urn with well-soaked florist's foam, leaving 2 inches extended above rim.
2. Insert, in order, white pine, boxwood, and holly branches, to establish dimensions of arrangement.
3. Add poinsettias, positioning largest flower in lower front of arrangement (refer to photograph for placement).
4. Using 19-gauge wire and floral tape, wire roses and insert throughout arrangement, above and below poinsettias.
5. Insert birch branches so that they extend beyond arrangement's parameters.
6. Tie a double-looped bow out of ribbon, attach to wired pick, and insert just right of center, at edge of urn.

VICTORIAN TABLETOP TREE

This ethereal tabletop tree embodies the magical spirit of Christmas—it's as if the angel might spread her wings and fly away at any moment, taking the little tree, light as air itself with its branches of baby's breath, with her. Fashioned as ornaments, the fragrant nosegays can be saved from year to year, or given as gifts.

Materials

5-foot-tall spruce tree (real or artificial)

2 strings of 30 electric-candle lights

1 large, Victorian-style angel tree-topper

Spool-wire

5 bunches baby's breath, glycerinized

16 nosegays (see page 188 for recipe)

Instructions

1. Place electric-candle lights on tree.
2. Anchor angel to top of tree.
3. Using spool-wire, attach nosegays to tree (refer to photograph for placement).
4. Fill in entire tree with pieces of baby's breath by simply pushing stems into open spaces.

VICTORIAN NOSEGAY ORNAMENTS

Imagine a group of nineteenth-century carolers, walking from house-to-house with nosegays such as these in hand, singing, "God rest ye, merry gentlemen," or "We wish you a merry Christmas!"

16 five-inch nosegay forms with white lace edging

16 florist's foam holders for nosegay forms

6 yards one-inch-wide pink-ribboned white lace

16 wired picks

19-gauge florist's wire

Dark green floral tape

Rose oil

16 sections of green ferns, glycerinized

AIR-DRIED FLOWERS:

36 pink larkspur pieces, each about 5 inches long (from whole stems broken into smaller lengths)

36 purple larkspur pieces, each about 5 inches long (from whole stems broken into smaller lengths)

48 pieces maroon crested cockscomb, from about 16 full flower heads

80 lavender stems

40 blue statice stems

32 white strawflowers

32 pale pink strawflowers

32 dark pink strawflowers

48 small heads gold yarrow

40 white pearly everlasting clusters of 2 to 3 stems each (ammobium or German statice may be substituted)

SILICA-DRIED FLOWERS:

16 'Bridal Pink' roses

22 purple button zinnias

21 maroon button zinnias

21 dark pink button zinnias

1. Insert florist's foam into nosegay forms.
2. Tie 16 four-inch bows from ribboned lace, attach to wired picks, and insert at bottom of florist's foam near form handles.
3. Using 19-gauge wire and floral tape, wire short stems for the fern sections, roses, and zinnias.
4. Fill outer edges of nosegay forms with fern pieces.
5. Create outlines with pink and purple larkspur pieces.
6. Insert a rose in the center of each form so that it extends 2 inches above florist's foam.
7. Place sections of cockscomb around each rose and throughout florist's foam.
8. Surround cockscomb with a mix of statice, strawflowers, and button zinnias.
9. Cover any open spaces with yarrow and pearly everlasting.
10. Add a drop or two of rose oil to each nosegay, for fragrance.

VICTORIAN-STYLE CHRISTMAS GARLAND

A handsome way to enhance embroidered silk stockings hung above the hearth is with a rich garland of silk roses, white strawflowers, and orange cockscomb. Luxe gold ribbon adds to the holiday splendor. All that's missing are some sugar cookies for Santa's arrival.

Materials

12-foot-long artificial spruce garland

10 yards gold ribbon—7 yards for wrapping garland; remainder for bows and streamers

2 two-inch-diameter needlepoint holders (pinholder cups)

2 small pieces Styrofoam

19-gauge florist's wire

Dark green floral tape

Spool-wire

Wire cutters

32 apricot silk roses (open flowers rather than buds)

26 white strawflowers, air-dried

30 golden orange crested cockscomb, air-dried

Instructions

1. Loosely wrap gold ribbon around garland and drape garland over top of mirror or on mantel.
2. Wire 2 bunches of strawflowers (each containing 9 stems) and tie with bows and streamers made from remaining gold ribbon. Attach one bunch to each end of garland with spool-wire.
3. Using 19-gauge wire and floral tape, wire stems for cockscomb and insert into garland (refer to photograph on following page for placement).
4. Fill both needlepoint holders with Styrofoam and position on mantel (shown here flanking the clock): If garland is resting on mantel, make a recessed area for each needlepoint holder.
5. With wire cutters, trim 20 silk-rose stems to lengths varying from 4 to 6 inches, so that roses can be mounted in needlepoint holders.
6. Add 4 strawflowers, with 4- to 5-inch stems, to each needlepoint "bouquet."
7. Scatter remaining 12 silk roses throughout garland, bending stems behind garland to hold them in place.

CHRISTMAS CAROUSEL HORSE

A carousel horse is a jolly reminder of sleigh rides and snowball fights and all the other joyful games that children play at Christmas. Here, the pony prances among gold balls and ivy vines, cinnamon sticks and pine branches.

Materials

Papier-mâché carousel horse: 14-inches tall, 16-inches long

Oblong basket with plastic liner: 21-inches long, 9-inches wide

Sheet moss

Hairpin hooks

6 blocks florist's foam

19-gauge florist's wire

Dark brown floral tape

22 long picks, or 18 picks and 4 dowels

4 gold Christmas balls

1 4-inch potted ivy plant

5 white pine branches, fresh

8 Red Delicious apples

12 hot red peppers

6 bunches oregano flowers, air-dried

6 gold yarrow, air-dried

6 pine cones

6 long cinnamon sticks

Instructions

1. Soak florist's foam in water until thoroughly wet. Place wet foam blocks in basket.
2. Push 4 long picks or dowels into bottoms of horse's feet and insert horse in florist's foam in center of basket.
3. Carve out a hole in left front corner of florist's foam and set potted ivy plant in it. Cover entire surface (of both pot and florist's foam) with sheet moss, securing with hairpin hooks (for instructions on how to make hooks, see page 200).
4. Insert white pine into florist's foam so that branches hang over edge of basket.
5. Poke picks into bottoms of apples and insert into florist's foam around horse's feet.
6. Place gold balls on picks and position throughout arrangement.
7. Using 19-gauge wire and floral tape, wire stems for oregano flowers and yarrow, and position around apples and gold balls.
8. Wire pine cones and insert into florist's foam at an angle so that some drape over edge of basket and some mingle around horse's feet (for instructions on how to wire pine cones, see page 200).
9. Using floral tape, attach picks to cinnamon sticks and scatter thoughout arrangement.
10. Using 19-gauge wire and floral tape, wire together bunches of hot peppers, 2 to 3 per group. Insert as accents, extending out from design.

A CHRISTMAS WISH

Star light, star bright: Make a Christmas wish, and blow out the candle on this elegant arrangement of red roses, green zinnias, and gilded holly leaves. A small table provides the perfect setting for this dramatic creation, which glitters with gold balls and ribbons.

Materials

10-inch-tall wooden candle-holder

1 candle adapter with fitted piece of florist's foam (available at craft and floral shops)

18-inch-long white taper

5 long wired picks

19-gauge florist's wire

Dark green floral tape

2 small bunches decorative green grapes

2 gold Christmas balls

2 yards gold roping

9 gilded holly leaves (available at craft stores, or coat leaves with gold spray-paint)

7 holly ferns, glycerinized

1 large bunch baby's breath, glycerinized

12 maroon 'Pavarotti' roses, silica-dried

6 'Envy' zinnias, silica-dried

Instructions

1. Fill candle adapter with florist's foam and place adapter in candleholder.
2. Push white taper into center of florist's foam.
3. Establish outline of arrangement by inserting holly ferns in a pyramid shape.
4. Attach decorative grape bunches to picks and insert into arrangement (refer to photograph for placement).
5. Attach gold balls to picks and insert left of center.
6. Tie a double bow from gold roping, attach to remaining pick, and insert under gold balls.
7. Using 19-gauge wire and floral tape, wire stems for roses and zinnias: Add roses throughout design, with largest rose towards bottom center of arrangement.
8. Insert zinnias between roses, following pyramid shape.
9. Wire and tape together clusters of baby's breath, and scatter throughout design.
10. Using 19-gauge wire and floral tape, wire holly leaves, and add to outer edges of arrangement.

HARK, THE HERALD ANGEL SINGS

An angel trumpets the good news—Gloria in excelsis Deo! This charming plaque was purchased at a crafts fair, and converted with flowers into a lovely door piece. Similar arrangements can be created using other holiday wall hangings, such as carved Santas or snowmen.

Materials

24-inch-high plywood angel plaque

1 piece Styrofoam: 2-inches thick, 4-inches long, 2-inches wide

Hot-glue gun and glue sticks

19-gauge wire

Dark green floral tape

1 can gold spray-paint

2 miniature holly branches, glycerinized

4 flat cedar branches, glycerinized

6 'Masterpiece' roses, silica-dried

Instructions

1. Coat miniature holly branches with gold spray-paint, and set aside to dry.
2. Using hot-glue gun, glue Styrofoam piece to center of back of plaque and let dry.
3. Working with angel right-side-up, insert cedar branches into Styrofoam in a flowing design (refer to photograph for placement).
4. Using 19-gauge wire and floral tape, wire roses and insert 3 into Styrofoam on either side of angel.
5. Add gold holly leaves as accents by inserting branches into Styrofoam under roses and on top of cedar on either side of angel.

WELCOME WREATH

Welcome visitors into your heart and your home with this cheerful cherub wreath. A frosting of blue in the spruce and hydrangea is fitting for the winter season. Sprayed with a few coats of sealer, the wreath will last through the cold weather.

Materials

18-inch-diameter blue spruce wreath

1 large cherub ornament

1 small cherub ornament

19-gauge florist's wire

Dark green floral tape

Spool-wire

9-foot-long segment of silver roping with tasseled ends

3 blue hydrangeas, silica-dried

5 dark red peonies, silica-dried

6 pink roses, silica-dried

Instructions

1. Attach cherubs to wreath with spool-wire, positioning large cherub on right side of wreath and small cherub on left.
2. Drape silver roping from left to right side of wreath, with tasseled ends hanging from right. Attach roping at left side with spool-wire, and drape ends around and behind large cherub on right side.
3. Using 19-gauge wire and floral tape, wire stems for the silica-dried flowers.
4. Attach hydrangea to wreath in a triangular pattern around small cherub on lefthand side (refer to photograph for placement).
5. Insert peonies above and below hydrangea, along curve of wreath.
6. Position roses on wreath toward outer edges of arrangement.

FLOWER-DRYING PANTRY

HOW TO MAKE HAIRPIN HOOKS

For each hairpin hook, bend a 4-inch length of 19-gauge florist's wire into a U-shape.

HOW TO WIRE DRIED FLOWERS

- Cut a 3-inch segment of dark green floral tape.
- Attach one end of the tape to the tip of a length of 19-gauge florist's wire, and pull it taut.
- Place the wire under the head of the dried flower, aligning it with the flower's 1-inch stem.
- Holding the wire and flower stem together with one hand, stretch the floral tape with the other, and twirl the wire to wrap it with the tape. The newly formed "stem" permits flexibility when arranging dried flowers.

HOW TO WIRE STRAWFLOWERS

- Strawflowers are wired before they are dried. Pick strawflowers when they are still in the bud stage.
- Cut the heads off the stems.
- Trim 19- or 20-gauge florist's wire to the desired "stem" length, and insert into base of the bud, in place of the actual stem.
- Place individually wired flowers upright in a container to air-dry.
- Allow to air-dry for two weeks: Buds will open and, in the process, secure themselves to the wire stems.

HOW TO WIRE PINE CONES

- Bend a 6- to 7-inch length of 19-gauge florist's wire into a loose curve.
- Work one end of the wire through the lowest scales of the pine cone, until it comes full circle.
- Secure wire around cone by twisting both ends together tightly.
- Use a wire-cutter to trim the new "stem" to the desired length.

DRYING APPLES

- Wash, core, and cut 'Red Delicious' apples into ¼-inch-thick slices.
- Dip slices into a one-to-one solution of fresh lemon juice and water, and place on a cookie sheet. Bake at 200°F, with the oven door slightly ajar, for eight to ten hours. Turn slices occasionally so that they bake evenly.
- Remove from oven and allow to cool. The slices may be strung alone or with bay leaves, or used as accents in dried creations.

DRYING ORANGES, LEMONS, AND LIMES

- To preserve oranges, lemons, and limes, cut fruit into slices about ¼-inch thick and place on top of a thin coating of silica gel on a cookie sheet.
- Bake at 200°F, with the oven door slightly ajar, for eight to ten hours. Turn slices occasionally so that they bake evenly.
- Remove from oven and, once slices have cooled, brush off any granules of silica gel.

DRYING POMEGRANATES AND ARTICHOKES

- Whole pomegranates and artichokes dry naturally in a few weeks.
- For ease in handling, and to facilitate arranging, insert a long wooden pick into the fresh stem.
- Place fruit on several sheets of paper toweling in a warm, dry area, such as the top of the refrigerator. Turn the fruit every few days.
- Over a period of about three weeks, the fruit will shrink and adhere to the pick.

BIBLIOGRAPHY

Docker, Amanda. *An English Country Lady's Book of Dried Flowers.* New York: Doubleday & Company, Inc., 1990.

Hillier, Malcolm. *Decorating with Dried Flowers.* New York: Crown Publishing, 1987.

Joosten, Titia. *Flower Drying with a Microwave.* Asheville, NC: Lark Books, 1988.

Karel, Leonard. *Dried Flowers from Antiquity to the Present.* Lanham, MD: Scarecrow Press, Inc., 1973.

Rountree, Susan H. *Christmas Decorations from Williamsburg.* Williamsburg, VA: Colonial Williamburg Foundation, 1991.

Schofield, Bernard. *A Miscellany of Garden Wisdom.* Philadelphia: Running Press, Inc., 1973.

Sheen, Joanna, and Caroline Alexander. *Dried Flower Gardening.* New York: Sterling Publishing Company, 1996.

MAIL-ORDER SOURCES

FERRY-MORSE SEEDS

P.O. Box 488
Fulton, KY 42041-0488
(800) 283-3400

FLOWER-DRI

Plantabbs Products
P.O. Box 397
Timonium, MD 21093
(800) 227-4340

GEORGE W. PARK SEED COMPANY, INC.

1 Parkton Avenue
Greenwood, SC 29647-0001
(800) 845-3369

GURNEY SEED AND NURSERY COMPANY

110 Capitol Street
Yankton, SD 57079
(605) 665-1671

HARRIS SEEDS

60 Saginaw Drive
Rochester, NY 14692-2960
(800) 514-4441

HENRY FIELD SEED AND NURSERY COMPANY

415 North Burnett
Shenandoah, IA 51602
(712) 246-2110

JACKSON & PERKINS

1 Rose Lane
Medford, OR 97501-9813
(800) 292-4769

JOHNNY'S SELECTED SEEDS

Foss Hill Road
Albion, ME 04910-9731
(207) 437-4301

SHEPHERD'S GARDEN SEEDS

30 Irene Street
Torrington, CT 06790
(860) 482-3638

SPRING HILL NURSERIES

6523 North Glanea Road
Peoria, IL 61632
(800) 582-8527

THOMPSON & MORGAN, INC.

P.O. Box 1308
Jackson, NJ 08527-0308
(800) 274-7333

W. ATLEE BURPEE CO.

300 Park Avenue
Warminster, PA 18974
(800) 487-5530

WAYSIDE GARDENS

1 Garden Lane
Hodges, SC 29695-0001
(800) 845-1124

COMMON NAME	BOTANICAL NAME	COMMON NAME	BOTANICAL NAME
ACACIA	*Acacia*	CORALBELLS	*Heuchera sanguinea*
ACROCLINIUM	*Helipterum roseum*	COREOPSIS	*Coreopsis tinctoria*
AGERATUM	*Ageratum houstonianum*	CORNFLOWER	*Centaurea cyanus*
AMARANTHUS	*Amaranthus caudatus*	COSMOS	*Cosmos bipinnatus*
AMMOBIUM	*Ammobium alatum*	COTONEASTER	*Cotoneaster*
ANDROMEDA	*Pieris japonica*	COTTON	*Gossypium*
APPLE	*Malus* species and hybrids	CRASPEDIA	*Craspedia globosa*
ARTEMISIA	*Artemisia ludoviciana*	CURLY WILLOW	*Salix matsudana* 'Tortuosa'
ARTICHOKE	*Cynara*	DAFFODIL	*Narcissus* species and hybrids
ASPIDISTRA	*Aspidistra elatior*	DAHLIA, dwarf	*Dahlia* hybrids
ASTER	*Aster novi-belgii*	DELPHINIUM	*Delphinium elatum*
ASTILBE	*Astilbe biternata* or *A. davidii*	DEUTZIA	*Deutzia*
AUSTRALIAN DAISY	*Ixodia achilloides*	DOCK	*Rumex crispus*
AZALEA	*Rhododendron*	DOGWOOD	*Cornus kousa* or *C. florida*
BABY'S BREATH	*Gypsophila paniculata*	DUSTY MILLER	*Senecio cineraria*
BACHELOR'S BUTTON	*Centaurea cyanus*	EDELWEISS	*Leontopodium alpinum*
BEARD GRASS	*Polypogon monspeliensis*	FALSE DRAGONHEAD	*Physostegia virginiana*
BEECH	*Fagus*	FALSE GOATSBEARD	*Astilbe davidii* or *A. biternata*
BEGONIA	*Begonia semperflorens*	FATSIA	*Fatsia japonica*
BELLS OF IRELAND	*Moluccella laevis*	FEVERFEW	*Tanacetum parthenium*
BITTERSWEET VINE	*Celastrus scandens*	FIRETHORN	*Pyracantha coccinea*
BLACKBERRY	*Rubus*	FLAT-LEAF CEDAR	*Chamaecyparis thyoides*
BLACK-EYED SUSAN	*Rudbeckia hirta* 'Gloriosa daisy'	FLOWERING QUINCE	*Chaenomeles speciosa*
BOXWOOD	*Buxus*	FORGET-ME-NOT	*Myosotis sylvatica*
BUNNY'S-TAIL GRASS	*Lagurus ovatus*	FORSYTHIA	*Forsythia* x *intermedia*
BURNING BUSH	*Euonymus atropurpurea*	FOXGLOVE	*Digitalis purpurea*
BUTTERCUP	*Ranunculus acris*	FUCHSIA	*Fuchsia* hybrids
CALENDULA	*Calendula officinalis*	GAY FEATHER	*Liatris spicata*
CAMPANULA	*Campanula*	GERANIUM, annual	*Pelargonium*
CANDYTUFT	*Iberis sempervirens*	GERANIUM, perennial	*Geranium* species and hybrids
CARNATION	*Dianthus caryophyllus*	GLOBE AMARANTH	*Gomphrena globosa*
CASPIA	*Limonium latifolium*	GLOBE THISTLE	*Echinops exaltatus*
CATTAIL	*Typha angustifolia*	GLORIOSA DAISY	*Rudbeckia hirta* 'Gloriosa daisy'
CHERRY	*Prunus*		
CHICKWEED	*Stellaria media*	GOLDENROD	*Solidago*
CHINESE LANTERN	*Physalis alkekengi*	HEATHER	*Calluna vulgaris*
CHIVE	*Allium schoenoprasum*	HEAVENLY BAMBOO	*Nandina domestica*
CHRYSANTHEMUM	*Dendranthemum* x *grandiflorum*	HOLLY FERN	*Polystichum*
CLARKIA	*Clarkia elegans*	HOLLYHOCK	*Alcea rosea*
COCKSCOMB, crested	*Celosia cristata*	HONESTY	*Lunaria annua* or *L. biennis*
COCKSCOMB, plumed, or feathered	*Celosia plumosa*	HONEY LOCUST	*Gleditsia triacanthos*
		HOP VINE	*Humulus lupulus*
COLUMBINE	*Aquilegia canadensis*	HORSE CHESTNUT	*Aesculus*
CONEFLOWER, purple	*Echinacea purpurea*	HYDRANGEA, bush	*Hydrangea macrophylla*

COMMON NAME	BOTANICAL NAME
HYDRANGEA, PEEGEE	*Hydrangea paniculata 'Grandiflora'*
HYDRANGEA, white, or snowball	*Hydrangea arborescens*
IMPATIENS	*Impatiens*
IRIS	*Iris* species and hybrids
IVY	*Hedera helix*
JAPANESE ANEMONE	*Anemone* x *hybrida*
JAPANESE HOLLY	*Ilex crenata*
JAPANESE PEONY	*Paeonia suffruticosa*
JOE-PYE WEED	*Eupatorium purpureum*
JOHNNY-JUMP-UP	*Viola tricolor*
LADY'S MANTLE	*Alchemilla mollis* or *A. vulgaris*
LAMB'S-EARS	*Stachys byzantina*
LARKSPUR	*Consolida ambigua*
LAUREL	*Laurus nobilis*
LAVENDER	*Lavandula* species and hybrids
LEMON	*Citrus limon*
LIATRIS	*Liatris spicata*
LILAC	*Syringa vulgaris*
LILY	*Lilium* hybrids
LILY-OF-THE-VALLEY	*Convallaria majalis*
LIME	*Citrus aurantifolia*
LOOSESTRIFE	*Lythrum*
LOVE-IN-A-MIST	*Nigella damascena*
LUPINE	*Lupinus*
MAIDENHAIR FERN	*Adiantum pedatum*
MAGNOLIA	*Magnolia grandiflora*
MAHONIA	*Mahonia*
MAPLE	*Acer*
MARIGOLD	*Tagetes* hybrids
MIMOSA	*Acacia*
MOCK ORANGE	*Philadelphus coronarius*
MONEY PLANT	*Lunaria annua* or *L. biennis*
MONKSHOOD	*Aconitum*
MORNING GLORY	*Ipomoea purpurea*
MOUNTAIN ASH	*Sorbus*
MULLEIN	*Verbascum*
NANDINA	*Nandina domestica*
OAK	*Quercus*
OAT GRASS	*Avena sativa*
ORANGE	*Citrus sinensis*
OREGANO	*Origanum vulgare*
OREGON GRAPE	*Mahonia*
ORIENTAL POPPY	*Papaver orientale*
OXEYE DAISY	*Leucanthemum vulgare*
PAMPAS GRASS	*Cortaderia selloana*
PANSY	*Viola* x *wittrockiana*
PARSLEY, CURLY	*Petroselinum crispum*

COMMON NAME	BOTANICAL NAME
PEARLY EVERLASTING	*Anaphalis margaritacea*
PEONY	*Paeonia* hybrids
PETUNIA	*Petunia*
PHLOX	*Phlox paniculata*
POMEGRANATE	*Punicum granatum*
POT MARIGOLD	*Calendula officinalis*
PURPLE CONEFLOWER	*Echinacea purpurea*
PUSSY WILLOW	*Salix discolor*
QUEEN ANNE'S LACE	*Daucus carota*
RANUNCULUS	*Ranunculus asiaticus*
RHODANTHE	*Helipterum roseum*
ROSE	*Rosa* species and hybrids
SALVIA, blue	*Salvia farinacea*
SEA LAVENDER	*Limonium latifolium*
SEDUM, 'Autumn joy'	*Hylotelephium telephium* x *H. spectabile*
SHASTA DAISY	*Leucanthemum* x *superbum*
SILVER-DOLLAR EUCALYPTUS	*Eucalyptus polyanthemos*
SILVER LACE VINE	*Polygonum aubertii*
SNAPDRAGON	*Antirrhinum majus*
SPEEDWELL	*Veronica* species and hybrids
SPIDER FLOWER	*Cleome hasslerana*
SPRENGERI FERN	*Asparagus densiflorus*
STARFLOWER	*Scabiosa stellata*
STATICE, annual	*Limonium sinuatum*
STATICE, German, or perennial	*Goniolimon tataricum*, or *Limonium tataricum*
STATICE, Russian, or rattail	*Psylliostachys suworowii*, or *Limonium suworowii*
STRAWFLOWER	*Helichrysum bracteatum*
SUNFLOWER	*Helianthus annuus*
SWEET ALYSSUM	*Lobularia maritima*
SWEET CORN	*Zea mays*
SWEET WILLIAM	*Dianthus barbatus*
TANSY	*Tanacetum vulgare*
TRUMPET VINE	*Campsis radicans*
TULIP	*Tulipa* hybrids
VERBENA	*Verbena* x *hortensis*
VERONICA	*Veronica* species and hybrids
VIBURNUM	*Viburnum prunifolium*
VIOLET	*Viola odorata*
WEIGELA	*Weigela florida*
WHEAT	*Triticum aestivum*
WINDFLOWER	*Anemone* species
WINGED EVERLASTING	*Ammobium alatum*
XERANTHEMUM	*Xeranthemum annuum*
YARROW	*Achillea millefolium* hybrids
ZINNIA	*Zinnia elegans* hybrids

BOTANICAL NAME	COMMON NAME	BOTANICAL NAME	COMMON NAME
Acacia	MIMOSA, or ACACIA	*Cleome hasslerana*	SPIDER FLOWER
Acer	MAPLE	*Consolida ambigua*	LARKSPUR
Achillea millefolium hybrids	YARROW	*Convallaria majalis*	LILY-OF-THE-VALLEY
Aconitum	MONKSHOOD	*Coreopsis tinctoria*	COREOPSIS
Adiantum pedatum	MAIDENHAIR FERN	*Cornus kousa*	DOGWOOD
Aesculus	HORSE CHESTNUT	*Cortaderia selloana*	PAMPAS GRASS
Ageratum houstonianum	AGERATUM	*Cosmos bipinnatus*	COSMOS
Alcea rosea	HOLLYHOCK	*Cotoneaster*	COTONEASTER
Alchemilla mollis or *A. vulgaris*	LADY'S MANTLE	*Craspedia globosa*	CRASPEDIA, DRUMSTICK
Allium schoenoprasum	CHIVE	*Cynara*	ARTICHOKE
Amaranthus caudatus	AMARANTHUS	*Dahlia* hybrids	DAHLIA, DWARF
Ammobium alatum	AMMOBIUM, WINGED EVERLASTING	*Daucus carota*	QUEEN ANNE'S LACE
Anaphalis margaritacea	PEARLY EVERLASTING	*Delphinium elatum*	DELPHINIUM
Anemone species	WINDFLOWER	*Dendranthemum* x *grandiflorum*	CHRYSANTHEMUM
Anemone x *hybrida*	JAPANESE ANEMONE	*Deutzia*	DEUTZIA
Antirrhinum majus	SNAPDRAGON	*Dianthus barbatus*	SWEET WILLIAM
Aquilegia canadensis	COLUMBINE	*Dianthus caryophyllus*	CARNATION
Artemisia ludoviciana	ARTEMISIA	*Digitalis purpurea*	FOXGLOVE
Asparagus densiflorus	SPRENGERI FERN	*Echinacea purpurea*	PURPLE CONEFLOWER
Aspidistra elatior	ASPIDISTRA	*Echinops exaltatus*	GLOBE THISTLE
Aster novi-belgii	ASTER	*Eucalyptus polyanthemos*	SILVER-DOLLAR EUCALYPTUS
Astilbe biternata or *A. davidii*	ASTILBE, FALSE GOATSBEARD	*Euonymus atropurpurea*	BURNING BUSH
Avena sativa	OAT GRASS	*Eupatorium purpureum*	JOE-PYE WEED
Begonia semperflorens	BEGONIA	*Fagus*	BEECH
Buxus	BOXWOOD	*Fatsia japonica*	FATSIA
Calendula officinalis	CALENDULA, POT MARIGOLD	*Forsythia* x *intermedia*	FORSYTHIA
Calluna vulgaris	HEATHER	*Fuchsia* hybrids	FUCHSIA
Campanula	CAMPANULA	*Geranium* species and hybrids	PERENNIAL GERANIUM
Campsis radicans	TRUMPET VINE	*Gleditsia triacanthos*	HONEY LOCUST
Celastrus scandens	BITTERSWEET VINE	*Gomphrena globosa*	GLOBE AMARANTH
Celosia cristata	CRESTED COCKSCOMB	*Goniolimon tataricum*	GERMAN, or PERENNIAL, STATICE
Celosia plumosa	PLUMED, or FEATHERED, COCKSCOMB	*Gossypium*	COTTON
Centaurea cyanus	BACHELOR'S BUTTON, CORNFLOWER	*Gypsophila paniculata*	BABY'S BREATH
Chaenomeles speciosa	FLOWERING QUINCE	*Hedera helix*	IVY
Chamaecyparis thyoides	FLAT-LEAF CEDAR	*Helianthus annuus*	SUNFLOWER
Citrus aurantifolia	LIME	*Helichrysum bracteatum*	STRAWFLOWER
Citrus limon	LEMON	*Helipterum roseum*	ACROCLINIUM, EVERLASTING, RHODANTHE
Citrus sinensis	ORANGE	*Heuchera sanguinea*	CORALBELLS
Clarkia elegans	CLARKIA	*Humulus lupulus*	HOP VINE
		Hydrangea arborescens	WHITE, or SNOWBALL HYDRANGEA